大学英语立体化网络化系列教材　　　　　　　　总主编　李淑静

③

博雅英语

BOYA College English

主　编：谭　颖
副主编：高　新　解阳平
编　者：李腊花　陈　龙　徐熙君
　　　　姚　伟　项景东　万　孜
审　校：Thomas Manson

北京大学出版社
PEKING UNIVERSITY PRESS

图书在版编目(CIP)数据

博雅英语.3 / 谭颖主编. —北京：北京大学出版社，2015.11
(大学英语立体化网络化系列教材)
ISBN 978-7-301-25415-8

Ⅰ.①博… Ⅱ.①谭… Ⅲ.①英语—高等学校—教材 Ⅳ.①H31

中国版本图书馆CIP数据核字(2015)第018126号

书　　名	博雅英语(3)
	BOYA YINGYU
著作责任者	谭　颖　主编
责任编辑	郝妮娜
标准书号	ISBN 978-7-301-25415-8
出版发行	北京大学出版社
地　　址	北京市海淀区成府路205号　100871
网　　址	http://www.pup.cn　新浪微博:@北京出版社
电子信箱	zbing@pup.pku.edu.cn
电　　话	邮购部 62752015　发行部 62750672　编辑部 62754382
印刷者	北京大学印刷厂
经销者	新华书店
	787毫米×1092毫米　16开本　11印张　420千字
	2015年11月第1版　2015年11月第1次印刷
定　　价	48.00元(配有光盘)

未经许可，不得以任何方式复制或抄袭本书之部分或全部内容。
版权所有，侵权必究
举报电话：010-62752024　电子信箱：fd@pup.pku.edu.cn
图书如有印装质量问题，请与出版部联系，电话：010-62756370

《博雅英语》专家委员会
（按姓氏拼音排列）

程朝翔　丁宏为　郭文革　胡壮麟
蒋学清　李淑静　林毅夫　凌　斌
刘意青　吕随启　申　丹　谭　颖
王义遒　张文霞　周小仪

前　言

古希腊罗马倡导的博雅教育(Liberal Education)，旨在传授广博的知识，培养独立完善的人格和优雅的气质，使人不仅获得专业技能，而且陶冶品学才识，成为完全的人。与之相辉映，中华文化传统如《论语》之"子曰：君子不器"，以及《大学》之"大学之道，在明明德，在亲民，在止于至善"，也强调人应该有完善的人格，不能像器具一样，只满足某一种用途。

北京大学教材建设委员会设立的大学英语教材改革项目《博雅英语》，正是要达到这样的目的，将大学英语课程的工具性和人文性有机统一，使之作为高等学校人文教育的一部分，体现高等教育的特点，以教材的思想性带动语言学习，不仅增强学生的英语综合应用能力和自主学习能力，而且发展学生的跨文化交际能力和批判性思维能力。

人文性目标首先体现在对教学材料的选择上。《博雅英语》通过走访人文社科领域学者和调研学习者需求，在选材上确定了"语言与文学、历史与文明、哲学与人生、建筑与艺术、法制与民主、经济与社会、人与自然、科技与教育"等八个主题板块。所选听读材料既有中西方经典作品或其介绍，也有对现实生活中普世热点问题的分析或讨论，力图达到经典与时代的结合、西方文化与中华文化的互动、人文素养与科学精神的交融，彰显教育的根本——立德树人，使学生在批判性的英语学习中，吸收优秀的文化、观念和正确的价值观，培养跨文化国际视野和中国情怀，树立文化自觉和文化自信，未来成为中外文化交流及"讲好中国故事、传播好中国声音、阐释好中国特色"的重要力量。

在教学材料的编排上，《博雅英语》遵循语言学习发展规律，力图贯彻"以输入为基础、以输出为驱动"的理念，注重经典阅读、培养思辨能力、强化书面及口头表达能力。每个主题单元都由四个板块构成：视听导入(Lead-in)、从读到写(Reading and Writing)、从读到说(Reading and Speaking)、跨文化交流(Cross Cultural Communication)，以听读促写、以听读促说、以英汉互译促跨文化学习及中国文化传播，融合听说读写译各种语言技能，促进学生综合语言应用能力的养成。在学习活动的设计中，《博雅英语》尤其注重开放性，启发学生对经典的感受能力，培养批判性思维习惯，引导学生主动学习、自主学习和个性化地学习，培养发现问题、分析问题、解决问题的创新能力。

《博雅英语》力求构建优质的教学资源共享体系，发挥好教材在引导教师转变教学观念、调整教学方式等方面的功能和作用。在提供学生用书、教师用书及相应的电子资源的同时，还将组织授课教师围绕教材的重点、难点、疑点或某些教学环节开发微课，以视频为主要载体记录并分享其教育教学活动的精彩，并通过开放性的网络平台鼓励师生共同构建教学资源，交流学习成果，营造出一个个真实的微教学资源环境和学习共同体。

在大学英语课程改革不断深化的新阶段，全体编者期望通过编写《博雅英语》，为丰富大学英语课程的人文内涵、实现其工具性与人文性的有机统一、促进学生的综合素质提高和全面发展尽自己的绵薄之力。不足之处难免，敬请批评指正。

李淑静
2015年5月

Contents

Unit 1 LANGUAGE AND LITERATURE 1
    Part One   Lead-in 2
                      Section 1   Listening: Nineteen Eighty-Four 2
                      Section 2   Watching: The Ancestor of Language 2
    Part Two   Reading and Writing 3
                      Text A   Words as Tools 3
    Part Three   Reading and Speaking 11
                      Text B   The Tower of Babel 11
    Part Four   Cross Cultural Communication 17
                      Passage A   我的童年 17
                      Passage B   The Dignity of Life and Death 18

Unit 2 HISTORY AND CIVILIZATION 21
    Part One   Lead-in 22
                      Section 1   Listening: American Indians 22
                  Section 2   Watching: Civilization in the West History 23
    Part Two   Reading and Writing 23
                  Text A   Greek Life—How The Greeks Lived 23
    Part Three   Reading and Speaking 32
                  Text B   Madness and Civilization 32
    Part Four   Cross Cultural Communication 38
                  Passage A   郑和下西洋——三保太监的不朽航程 38
                  Passage B   The First Voyage—Discovery of the New Land ... 40

Unit 3 PHILOSOPHY AND LIFE 42
    Part One   Lead-in 43
                  Section 1   Listening: True Success 43
                  Section 2   Watching: Less Stuff, More Happiness 44
    Part Two   Reading and Writing 44
                  Text A   Two Truths to Live By 44
    Part Three   Reading and Speaking 52
                  Text B   What is Enough? The Race for More 52
    Part Four   Cross Cultural Communication 57

		Passage A 人生的爱好者：陶渊明 ·· 57
		Passage B Henry David Thoreau ·· 58

Unit 4 ART AND ARCHITECTURE ··· 61

Part One	Lead-in ··· 62	
	Section 1 Listening: Architecture and Art ·································· 62	
	Section 2 Watching: The Chinese Temples Architecture ······· 62	
Part Two	Reading and Writing ··· 63	
	Text A Art Is Universal ·· 63	
Part Three	Reading and Speaking ·· 72	
	Text B Buildings and Culture Produce Architecture ············ 72	
Part Four	Cross Cultural Communication ··· 77	
	Passage A 舞蹈的建筑 ··· 77	
	Passage B Hagia Sophia ·· 79	

Unit 5 DEMOCRACY AND LAW ··· 82

Part One	Lead-in ··· 83	
	Section 1 Listening: The Founding Principles of American Democracy ·································· 83	
	Section 2 Watching: American Election ··································· 83	
Part Two	Reading and Writing ··· 84	
	Text A The State and the Individual ·· 84	
Part Three	Reading and Speaking ·· 93	
	Text B Give Me Liberty or Give Me Death ··························· 93	
Part Four	Cross Cultural Communication ··· 99	
	Passage A 贤能政府 ··· 99	
	Passage B Resistance to Civil Government ···························· 101	

Unit 6 ECONOMY AND SOCIETY ·· 104

Part One	Lead-in ·· 105	
	Section 1 Listening: The Ice Bucket Challenge ······················ 105	
	Section 2 Watching: Should You Donate Differently? ········ 105	
Part Two	Reading and Writing ··· 106	
	Text A The "Dematerialization" of Society in the Digital Age ·· 106	
Part Three	Reading and Speaking ·· 115	
	Text B Lost Generation: Pain of Privilege and Plight of the Poor ·· 115	

Contents

Part Four	Cross Cultural Communication	120
	Passage A 给自己一个梦想	120
	Passage B Integrity	121

Unit 7 MAN AND NATURE ... 124

Part One	Lead-in	125
	Section 1 Listening: Plant Life	125
	Section 2 Watching: Understanding the Natural World	126
Part Two	Reading and Writing	126
	Text A Natural Selection	126
Part Three	Reading and Speaking	135
	Text B Nature	135
Part Four	Cross Cultural Communication	140
	Passage A 老子的智慧	140
	Passage B Remarks at Paris Summit on Climate Change	142

Unit 8 SCIENCE AND EDUCATION ... 146

Part One	Lead-in	147
	Section 1 Listening: Technology Abuse	147
	Section 2 Watching: Technology's Epic Story	148
Part Two	Reading and Writing	148
	Text A Scientific Education	148
Part Three	Reading and Speaking	157
	Text B Man or Machine? The Age of the Robot Blurs Sci-fi and Cutting-edge Science	157
Part Four	Cross Cultural Communication	163
	Passage A 万世师表,以德服人	163
	Passage B The Socratic Quest for Wisdom	164

Unit 1

LANGUAGE AND LITERATURE

Every word in a language has some job to do, but no two of them have exactly the same job or even the same kind of job. Words are like tools in a tool kit. Just as each tool is used to do a different job—you don't do with a hammer the same thing you do with a wrench—so different kinds of words perform different tasks.

—From *An Introduction to Philosophical Analysis* by John Hospers

And the whole earth was of one language, and of one speech.

—From *The Language Instinct*

Learning Objectives

Upon the completion of this unit, you should be able to

Remembering & Understanding	★ read Text A and Text B aloud smoothly with expression indicative of comprehension and tone; ★ identify and explain in your own words the thesis and the major points of Text A and Text B;
Analyzing & Applying	★ learn to use affixes to enlarge your vocabulary; ★ make reference to the thesis and/or the major points of Text A and Text B in your writing; ★ produce sentences with attributive clauses to make expressions cohesive;
Evaluating & Creating	★ adopt relevant writing strategies in definition paragraphs; ★ reflect on the thesis and major points of Text B and develop your critical thinking; ★ deliver a clear and coherent oral presentation of your views on the relationship between human-beings and language.

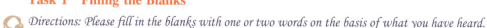

Section 1　Listening: Nineteen Eighty-Four

Task 1　Filling the Blanks

Directions: Please fill in the blanks with one or two words on the basis of what you have heard.

　　Nineteen Eighty-Four is one of Orwell's most powerful _____ novels, a beautifully crafted warning against the dangers of a totalitarian society, and one of the most famous novels in the dystopian genre. Winston Smith is a low-ranking member of the ruling party in London whose every move is _____ by telescreens. Everywhere Winston goes, the party's omniscient leader, Big Brother, watches him. The party is trying to eradicate the possibility of political rebellion by _____ all words related to it from the language, creating sanitized "Newspeak." "Thoughtcrime" (thinking rebellious thoughts) is illegal. Winston, who works at the Ministry of Truth altering historical records for the party's benefit, is frustrated and oppressed by the _____ on free thought, sex and individuality. He illegally _____ a diary to record his thoughts and spends his evenings wandering the poor areas where the "proles" live, relatively free from monitoring. Winston starts an illicit affair with Julia, a fellow party employee, but they are caught by a party spy, and in Room 101, Winston is forced to _____ his worst fear. Giving up his love for Julia in terror, Winston is released, his spirit broken and his acceptance of the party complete.

　　In 1949, at the beginning of the nuclear age and before television was _____, Orwell's creation of a telescreen-monitored world just a single generation into the future was terrifying. This is an important novel not only for its stark warning against _____ authority (and its somewhat ironic contribution to modern television content), but also for its insights into the power of _____ language, history, and the psychology of fear and control. These issues are perhaps even more _____ today than when Orwell penned his novel.

Task 2　Group Discussion

Directions: Please discuss the following questions in pairs or groups based on what you have heard.

1. According to the audio clip, what kind of novel is *Nineteen Eighty-Four* labeled as?
2. What is the novel *Nineteen Eighty-Four* mainly about?
3. Why is the novel *Nineteen Eighty-Four* regarded by the speaker as an important one?

Section 2　Watching: The Ancestor of Language

Task 1　Group Discussion

Directions: Please watch the video clip "The Ancestor of Language" and discuss the three questions below in pairs or groups.

1. How does the speaker think about the distant relationships among human languages?
2. According to Murray Gell-Mann, when can modern languages at least trace their history back to?
3. What is called a bottleneck in Murray Gell-Mann's talk?

Task 2 Summarizing

Directions: Please watch the video again, and try to summarize the main idea.

Part Two   Reading and Writing

Text A

Words as Tools
John Hospers

1. Just as we use nouns to *stand for* kinds of things (not individual things, except in the case of proper names), so we use adjectives to stand for kinds of qualities: "sweet," "*sour*," "dark," "heavy," "smooth," "reticulated(网状的)," and so on. "Dark" may be dark brown, dark blue, dark green, or dark red, but the adjective "dark" applies to them all: we have one word and many different *equalities* united by a certain *similarity*.

2. Adverbs are words that are used to describe ways of behaving or doing: "*swiftly*," "*greedily*," "*hastily*," "lovingly," "haltingly," "slowly," "*deliberately*." Again, each of these adverbs is used not only to describe the manner of this particular action but the manner of countless others that have some similarity to it. "Slowly" can describe how a person walks, how she pronounces her words, how she eats her food, and so on.

3. Prepositions refer to certain relations that things have to one another: "above," "below," "inside," "outside," "between," "beyond."

4. Verbs stand for different kinds of action or *initiation* of change: "eat," "run," "*slide*," "*accelerate*," "fly," "stop."

5. Conjunctions do not describe any features of the world but indicate how various clauses in a sentence are related to one another: "He and she will go" has a different meaning from "He or she will go." "Stop or I'll scream" is the same as "If you don't stop, I'll scream," but different from "Stop and I'll scream."

6. Interjections are used to express a person's attitude toward something — they don't describe the thing, they express how we feel toward it: "alas(唉)," "hurrah(万岁)," "dammit(该死)," "whoopee(欢呼声)." (We can express our feelings in many other ways as well.)

7. When a word is used to name a class of things, the word is like the *label* on a bottle. The label tells you what's in the bottle, and if two bottles have different kinds of contents, it is important not to use the same label for both of them. The label has no importance in itself; it only indicates what is in the bottle. Labels, of course, can be written in different languages yet still be labels for the same kind of things. They can

also be either heard (if *oral*) or seen (if written). *Either way*, having words saves us *enormous* labor: instead of going to the thing, giraffe, we can mention the word, "giraffe," and other people who understand the English language will know what we mean.

8   "A word is only a sign." But it isn't a natural sign, the way a twister in the sky is the sign of a tornado（龙卷风）or falling barometric pressure（气压）is the sign of an *approaching* storm. These signs occur in nature, and human beings had to discover what they are and act accordingly. We could not turn them around and change them, since they are not man-made. But words, like the notes on a musical staff, are *conventional* signs: this word stands for this class of things, this note on the staff stands for this class of sound pitches. In natural signs, A *signifies* B *regardless of* what human beings believe or decide; in conventional signs, human beings decide which A's will be used to stand for which B's.

9   As we have seen, however, not all words are the names of classes of things (nouns) or even classes of actions (verbs) or classes of qualities (adjectives). Every word in a language has some job to do, but no two of them have exactly the same job or even the same kind of job. Words are like tools in a tool kit. Just as each tool is used to do a different job—you don't do with a *hammer* the same thing you do with a wrench（扳手）—so different kinds of words perform different tasks. Pronouns, for example, are *substitutes* for nouns, except that "I" always refers to whomever is speaking and "you" refers to whomever is being spoken to. To know the meaning of a word is to know what kind of job it does, what its function is in the language.

10 When do we know the meaning of a word or phrase? When we know the rule for its use—that is, when we know under what conditions the word is to be used, when the word is *applicable* to a given situation, and when it is not. Usually when we ask for the rule for the use of a word, we are asking for the *definition* of the word.

11 A definition of a word tells us what *characteristics* (features, qualities, *properties*—all these words are used, and philosophers often draw distinctions among them) something has to have in order for the word to apply to it. The word "triangle" means any plane closed figure *bounded* by three straight lines. It is defined in terms of these three features. Each of the three is a "defining feature: that is, something wouldn't be a triangle if it lacked any one of them. And the three together give us the definition: the word is applicable to whatever has these three characteristics and to nothing that does not have them.

12 A word is said to *designate* the sum of the characteristics that something must have in order for the word to be applicable to it. The word "triangle" designates the properties of being three-sided, closed, and two-dimensional. These three are *sufficient* to define the word, as it is used in the English language. This definition *distinguishes* triangles from everything that is not a triangle.

13 In daily life, when we call something by a certain name we don't usually bother to say which features are defining (at least as we are using the word) and which ones are

not. Would you still call this a table if you painted it a different color? Of course; so the color is not defining. Would you still say it was a table if you could *petrify* it (turn it into stone)? Yes, as long as it continued to have a top and legs to support it. Would you say it was still a table if you cut off the legs? Here we might not be sure; but if it had no legs but hung by a chain from the ceiling, and we could still use it to read and write by, and to serve meals on, probably we would still call it a table; in that case, having legs would not be a defining feature of a table.

New Words

sour	[saʊr]	*a.*	having a sharp biting taste 酸的
equality	[iˈkwɑːləti]	*n.*	the quality of being the same in quantity or measure or value or status 同等，平等
similarity	[ˌsɪməˈlærɪti]	*n.*	the quality of being similar 相似性
swiftly	[ˈswɪftlɪ]	*ad.*	in a swift manner 迅速地，敏捷地
greedily	[ˈgridɪlɪ]	*ad.*	in a greedy manner 贪心地，贪婪地
hastily	[ˈhestɪlɪ]	*ad.*	in a hurried or hasty manner 匆忙地，仓促地
deliberately	[dɪˈlɪbərɪtlɪ]	*ad.*	in a deliberate unhurried manner 深思熟虑地
initiation	[ɪˌnɪʃɪˈeʃən]	*n.*	the act of starting something for the first time 起始
slide	[slaɪd]	*v.*	move obliquely or sideways, usually in an uncontrolled manner 滑落
accelerate	[ækˈsɛləˌret]	*v.*	move faster 加速
label	[ˈleɪbl]	*n.*	brief description given for purposes of identification 标签
oral	[ˈɔrəl]	*a.*	using speech rather than writing 口头的
enormous	[ɪˈnɔːrməs]	*a.*	extraordinarily large in size or extent or amount or power or degree 巨大的
approaching	[əˈprotʃɪŋ]	*a.*	of the relatively near future 逼近的
conventional	[kənˈvɛnʃənəl]	*a.*	following accepted customs and proprieties 传统的；常用的
signify	[ˈsɪgnəˌfaɪ]	*v.*	convey or express a meaning 意味；预示
hammer	[ˈhæmɚ]	*n.*	a hand tool with a heavy rigid head and a handle; used to deliver an impulsive force by striking 锤子
substitute	[ˈsʌbstɪtuːt]	*n.*	a person or thing that takes or can take the place of another 替代物
applicable	[ˈæplɪkəbəl]	*a.*	capable of being applied; having relevance 适当的；可应用的
definition	[ˌdɛfəˈnɪʃən]	*n.*	a concise explanation of the meaning of a word or phrase or symbol 定义
characteristics	[ˌkærɪktəˈrɪstɪks]	*n.*	a distinguishing quality 特性

property	[ˈprɑːpərti]	n.	a basic or essential attribute shared by all members of a classs 属性
bounded	[ˈbaʊndɪd]	a.	having the limits or boundaries established 有界限的
designate	[ˈdɛzɪɡˌnet]	v.	indicate a place, direction, person, or thing; either spatially or figuratively 指明, 指出
sufficient	[səˈfɪʃənt]	a.	of a quantity that can fulfill a need or requirement but without being abundant 足够的; 充足的
distinguish	[dɪˈstɪŋɡwɪʃ]	v.	mark as different 区分, 辨别
petrify	[ˈpɛtrəˌfaɪ]	v.	change into stone 石化

Phrases & Expressions

stand for	represent 代表, 代替; 象征
either way	no matter how, one way or the other 无论哪种方式
regardless of	despite of 不管, 不顾

Notes

1. The passage is adapted from the book *An Introduction to Philosophical Analysis* by John Hospers.
2. John Hospers (June 9, 1918 — June 12, 2011) was an American philosopher and politician. Graduated from Central College, Hospers earned advanced degrees from the University of Iowa and Columbia University. He conducted research, wrote, and taught in areas of philosophy, including aesthetics and ethics. He taught philosophy at Brooklyn College and at the University of Southern California, where for many years he was chairman of the philosophy department and professor emeritus.

Task 1 Generating the Outline

Directions: Please identify the thesis of the passage and the main point of each paragraph, and then find out how these points develop the thesis. You may use the table below for your help.

Para. 1: The definition	Nouns stand for _____ ; adjectives stand for _____ . We have one word and many different equalities united by _____ .
Para. 2: The definition	Adverbs are used to describe _____ . Many adverbs are used not only to describe the manner of _____ but the manner of countless others that have _____ to it.
Para. 3: The definition	Prepositions refer to _____ that things have to one another.

Para. 4: The definition	Verbs stand for _____ or _____.
Para. 5: The definition	Conjunctions do not describe _____, but indicate how _____ in a sentence are related to one another.
Para. 6: The definition	Interjections are used to express _____ — they don't describe the thing, they express _____.
Para. 7: The analogy	When a word is used to name a class of things, the word is like _____ on a bottle.
Para. 8: The contrast	Words are not _____ signs. They are _____ signs.
Para. 9: The analysis	Every word in a language has some job to do, but no two of them have _____ job or even _____ job. Different kinds of words _____ different tasks. To know the meaning of a word is to know _____.
Para. 10: The explanation	When we know _____, we know the meaning of a word or phrase.
Para. 11: The analysis	Word is applicable to whatever has the three characteristics— _____, _____, _____, and to nothing that does not have them.
Para. 12: The analysis	A word is said to _____ the sum of the characteristics that something must have in order for the word to be applicable to it.
Para. 13: The conclusion	In daily life, when we call something by a certain name while we don't say _____ and _____.

Task 2 Understanding the Text

Directions: Please answer the following questions based on Text A.

1. What do we use nouns and adjectives to stand for respectively?
2. What can the word "swiftly" be used to describe? Please give some examples.
3. Can conjunctive words be used to describe anything? If Hcy can't, then what's their function?
4. What's the *part of speech*(词性) of the word "oops"?
5. What's the meaning of "The label has no importance in itself; it only indicates what is in the bottle" in Paragraph 7?
6. Why does the author take "twister" as an example in Paragraph 8?
7. What's the difference between natural signs and conventional signs?
8. When do we know the meaning of a word or phrase?
9. What does "defining feature" in Paragraph 11 refer to?
10. Why does the author take "table" as an example in the last paragraph?

Task 3 Vocabulary Building

Directions: A common way to form an abstract noun is to add the suffix -ity to an adjective. For example:

equal + ity → equality   similar + ity → similarity

Study the following abstract nouns formed by adding -ity to adjectives and complete the following sentences with them. Change the form where necessary.

> capability   complexity   curiosity   publicity   rapidity   responsibility

1. What is curious is the _____ with which the new phrase has spread in America.
2. The most widely used opportunities of generating _____ are sponsoring cultural activities.
3. He had the _____ of completing the job in the given time.
4. He challenges every standard and method in his sphere of _____.
5. His _____ prompted him to ask questions.
6. Scientists are continuing to discover new ranks of soldiers in the immune system army and to observe greater _____ in its maneuvers.

Directions: The prefix pre- with the meaning of "before" can be added to nouns, verbs and adjectives with or without the hyphen. For example:

Pre- + position → preposition   pre- + school → preschool

Study the following words formed by adding pre- to nouns, verbs and adjectives and complete the following sentences with them. Change the form where necessary.

> preexist   prehistoric   premature   prenuptial   preplan   presuppose

1. There is growing concern about the increase in the number of _____ agreements.
2. It's dangerous to _____ that a person is guilty.
3. Most scientists think that _____ people used the pieces of ochre to draw symbolic decorations on their bodies.
4. Earthquake emergency _____ is a guiding principle for earthquake emergency response.
5. Throughout the classical period they believed that man does not create the mathematical facts; they _____. He is limited to ascertaining and recording them.
6. She had been perturbed by the _____ announcement of his engagement.

Task 4 Learning the Phrases

Directions: Please fill in the blanks of the sentences below with the phrases listed in the box. Change the forms if necessary. Notice that some phrases need to be used more than once.

> stand for   occur in   regardless of
> distinguish... from...   in terms of   apply to

1. A lot of students, _____ on campus, will work at some of the eateries on campus.
2. A friend is a friend, a foe is a foe; one must clearly _____ a friend _____ a foe.
3. Well, I know F. P. A. _____ free of particular average.

4. Advanced international technologies should be introduced, digested and absorbed to _____ the Olympics.
5. How many times does the word "the" _____ the sentence you are reading?
6. He _____ freedom of speech for everyone _____ color, race or creed.
7. Such incidents do not often _____ her novels; their tone is reserved.
8. Please think of your priorities not _____ what activities you do, but when you do them.
9. International students can also _____ become resident assistants after a year in the dorms.

Task 5   Studying the Sentence Structure
Sentences with attributive clause
Sentences from the text
1. Adverbs are words that are used to describe ways of behaving or doing. (Para. 2)
2. Prepositions refer to certain relations that things have to one another. (Para. 3)
3. ...the word is applicable to whatever has these three characteristics and to nothing that does not have them...(Para. 11)
4. A word is said to designate the sum of the characteristics that something must have in order for the word to be applicable to it. (Para. 12)

Directions: Please follow the examples and create five sentences with attributive clause on your own.
Tips
1. In writing, two sentences can be combined into one by making one of them an attributive clause in the new sentence.
2. The two sentences must have at least one thing in common. For example, the subject Jane constitutes the shared element between sentence A "Jane is a woman." and sentence B "She loves her children very much." Thus they can be combined into one sentence with an attributive clause "Jane is a woman who loves her children very much."

1. _____
   _____.
2. _____
   _____.
3. _____
   _____.
4. _____
   _____.
5. _____
   _____.

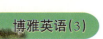

Task 6 Paraphrasing Difficult Sentences

1. Again, each of these adverbs is used not only to describe the manner of this particular action but the manner of countless others that have some similarity to it.
   _____
   _____.

2. In natural signs, A signifies B regardless of what human beings believe or decide; in conventional signs, human beings decide which A's will be used to stand for which B's.
   _____
   _____.

3. Words are like tools in a tool kit. Just as each tool is used to do a different job—you don't do with a hammer the same thing you do with a wrench—so different kinds of words perform different tasks.
   _____
   _____.

4. When we know the rule for its use—that is, when we know under what conditions the word is to be used, when the word is applicable to a given situation, and when it is not.
   _____
   _____.

5. Here we might not be sure; but if it had no legs but hung by a chain from the ceiling, and we could still use it to read and write by, and to serve meals on, probably we would still call it a table; in that case, having legs would not be a defining feature of a table.
   _____
   _____.

Task 7 Summarizing the Text

Directions: Please summarize text A in about 150 words. You may use the table in Task 1 to help you.

Task 8 Writing with Definition

Directions: Write three paragraphs by using definition on the topic of how words help us convey meaning. In the first paragraph you need to give some specific definition of a word and its function. In the last paragraph, you should try to summarize the reasons why and the ways that words can help us communicate. Your writing should be about 200 words. You may use what is provided below in the box for your help.

Tips

1. Whenever we attempt to answer questions like "what is a giraffe," "what is tornado," and "what is triangle," we are trying to provide a definition to these terms or concepts. In a piece of writing, we also need to provide definitions to words, terms, and concepts under discussion. However, while some questions may be easy to answer, other questions are difficult to handle, since they concern profound ideas about which opinions differ. Usually, one person's definition of a certain concept shows that person's special understanding or opinion of that concept.

2. Generally, definition is a statement giving the meaning of a word or expression. It is supposed to be clear and distinct. And it is a logical support in our writing.

3. A definition is basically composed of three parts: the first is the term or concept to be defined — the target of the definition; the second is the general category the target belongs to; the third is the distinguishing feature or features that characterize the target.
4. A good definition meets four criteria:
   a) The definition provides the correct general category of the target, being neither too large nor too small.
   b) The definition provides the correct distinguishing feature or features that accurately describe the unique characteristics of the target.
   c) The definition does not use an example as an explanation.
   d) The definition is not circular, that is, it does not explain the word with another form of the same word.

> A word is only a sign [...]
> For example, the "sweet" stands for kinds of qualities [...]
> Words are like tools in a tool kit [...]

Part Three Reading and Speaking

Text B

The Tower of Babel
Steven Pinker

1   And the whole earth was of one language, and of one speech. And it came to pass, as they journeyed from the east, that they found a plain in the land of Shinar（希纳尔）; and they *dwelt* there. And they said to one another, Go to, let us make brick, and burn them *thoroughly.* And they had bricks for stone, and slime（黏液）had they for mortar（灰浆）. And they said, Go to, let us build as a city and a tower, whose top may reach unto heaven; and let us make us a name, *lest* we be *scattered* abroad upon the face of the whole earth. And the Lord came down to see the city and the tower, which the children of men built. And the Lord said, Behold, the people is one, and they have all one language; and this they begin to do: and now nothing will be *restrained* from them, which they have imagined to do, Go to, let us go down, and there *confound* their language, that they may not understand one another's speech. So the Lord scattered them abroad *from thence* upon the face of all the earth; and they *left off* to build the city. Therefore is the name of it called *Babel*; because the Lord did there confound the language of all the earth; and from thence did the Lord scatter them abroad upon the face of all the earth. (Genesis 11:1–9)

2   In the year of our Lord 1957, the linguist Martin Joos *reviewed* the preceding three decades of research in linguistics and *concluded* that God had actually gone much further in confounding the language of descendants. Whereas the God of Genesis was said to *be content with* mere mutual unintelligibility（晦涩难懂）, Joos *declared* that "language could differ from each other without limit and in unpredictable ways." That same year, the Chomskyan revolution began with the publication of *Syntactic Structures*, and the next three decades took us back to the literal *biblical* account. According to Chomsky, a visiting Martian scientist would surely conclude that *aside from* their mutually unintelligible vocabularies, Eearthlings speak a single language.

3   Even by the standards of theological debates, these *interpretations* are strikingly different. Where did they come from? The 4,000 to 6,000 languages of the planet do look impressively different from English and from one another. Here are the most conspicuous ways in which languages can differ from what we are used to in English:

1. English is an "isolating" language which builds sentences by rearranging immutable word-sized units, like *Dog bites man* and *Man bites dog*. Other languages express who did what to whom by *modifying* nouns with case affixes, or by modifying the verb with affixes that agree with its role-players in number, *gender* and person. One example is Latin, an "inflecting" language in which each affix contains several pieces of information; another is Kivunjo, an "agglutinating"（粘合的）language in which each affix conveys one piece of information and many affixes are strung together.

2. English is a "fixed-word-order" language where each phrase has a fixed position. "Free-word-order" languages allow phrase order to vary. In an extreme case like the Australian *aboriginal* language Warlpiri（瓦尔皮里语）, words from different phrases can be scrambled together: *This man speared a kangaroo* can be expressed as *Man this kangaroo speared, Man kangaroo speared this,* and any of the other four orders, all completely synonymous.

3. English is an "accusative（宾格的）" language, where the subject of an intransitive verb, like *she* in *She ran*, is treated identically to the subject of a transitive verb, like *she* in *She kissed Larry*, and different from the object of the transitive verb, like *her* in *Larry kissed her*. "Ergative" languages like Basque（巴斯克语）and many Australian languages have a different *scheme* for collapsing these three roles. The subject of an intransitive verb and the object of a transitive verb are identical, and the subject of the transitive is the one that behaves differently. It is as if we were to say *Ran her* to mean "She ran."

4. English is a "subject-*prominent*" language in which all sentences must have a subject (even if there is nothing for the subject to refer to, as in *It is raining* or *There is a unicorn in the garden*). In "topic-prominent" languages like Japanese, sentences have a special position that is filled by the current topic of the conversation, as in *This place, planting wheat is good* or *California, climate is good*.

5. English is an "SVO" language, with the order subject-verb-object (*Dog bites man*). Japanese is subject-object-verb (SOV: *Dog man bites*); Modern Irish is verb-subject-

object (VSO: *Bites dog man*).

6. In English, a noun can name a thing in any *construction*: *a banana, two bananas; any banana; all the bananas*. In "classifier" languages, nouns fall into gender classes like human, animal, inanimate, one-dimensional, two-dimensional, cluster, tool, food, and so on. In many constructions, the name for the class, not the noun itself, must be used—for example, three hammers would be referred to as *three tools, to wit hammer*....

4   God did not have to do much to confound the language of Noah's descendants. *In addition to* vocabulary—whether the word for "mouse" is *mouse* or *souris*—a few *properties* of language are simply not *specified* in Universal Grammar and can vary as parameters （参数）. For example, it is up to each language to choose whether the order of *elements* within a phrase is head-first or head-last (*eat sushi* and *to Chicago* versus *sushi eat* and *Chicago to*) and whether a subject is mandatory in all sentences or can be *omitted* when the speaker desires. Furthermore, a particular grammatical widget often does a great deal of important work in one language and hums away unobtrusively（不显眼的）in the corner of another. The *overall* impression is that Universal Grammar is like an archetypal（原型的）body plan found across vast numbers of animals in a phylum（门）. For example, among all the amphibians, reptiles, birds and mammals, there is a common body architecture, with a segmented backbone, four jointed *limbs*, a tail, a skull, and so on. The various parts can be grotesquely distorted or stunted（发育不良的）across animals: a bat's wing is a hand, a horse trots on its middle toes, whales' forelimbs have become flippers（蹼）and their hindlimbs have shrunken to invisible nubs（块）, and the tiny hammer, anvil（砧骨）, and stirrup（镫骨）of the mammalian middle ear are jaw parts of reptiles. But from newts（蝾螈）to elephants, a common topology（解剖学）of the body plan—the shin bone connected to the thigh bone, the thigh bone connected to the hip bone—can be discerned. Many of the differences are caused by minor variations in the relative timing and rate of growth of the parts during embryonic（胚胎的）development. Differences among languages are similar. There seems to be a common plan of syntactic（句法的）, morphological（形态学的）, and phonological（音韵学的）rules and principles, with a small set of varying parameters, like a checklist of options. Once set, a parameter can have far-reaching changes on the *superficial* appearance of the language.

New Words

dwell	[dwɛl]	v.	inhabit or live in 居住
thoroughly	[ˈθʌrəli]	ad.	in a complete and thorough manner 彻底地,完全地
lest	[lɛst]	conj.	to prevent 以防
scatter	[ˈskætɚ]	v.	cause to separate 分散,散开
restrain	[rɪˈstren]	v.	keep under control; keep in check 抑制,控制
confound	[kənˈfaʊnd]	v.	be confusing or perplexing to; cause to be unable to think clearly 使混淆,使混乱
Babel	[ˈbebl]	n.	a tower built by Noah's descendants (probably in Babylon) who intended it to reach up to heaven; 巴别塔,通天塔
review	[rɪˈvju]	v.	to think about past events; to write a report of a book in which you give your opinion of it. 回顾,评估
conclude	[kənˈklud]	v.	draw or come to a conclusion 推断,作结论
declare	[dɪˈklɛr]	v.	state emphatically and authoritatively 声明,宣称
biblical	[ˈbɪblɪkl]	a.	of or pertaining to or contained in or in accordance with the Bible 圣经的,依据圣经的
interpretation	[ɪnˌtɚprɪˈteʃən]	n.	an explanation of something 解释
modify	[ˈmɑdɪfaɪ]	v.	add a modifier to a constituent 修饰
gender	[ˈdʒɛndɚ]	n.	a grammatical category in inflected languages governing the agreement between nouns and pronouns and adjectives 性(语法上的)
aboriginal	[ˌæbəˈrɪdʒənl]	a.	of or pertaining to members of the indigenous people of Australia(澳大利亚)土著的
scheme	[skiːm]	n.	a group of independent but interrelated elements comprising a unified whole 体制
prominent	[ˈprɑmɪnənt]	a.	having a quality that thrusts itself into attention 突出的,显著的
construction	[kənˈstrʌkʃən]	n.	a group of words that form a constituent of a sentence and are considered as a single unit 句子
property	[ˈprɑpɚti]	n.	the ways in which a substance or object behaves in particular conditions 特性
specify	[ˈspɛsɪfaɪ]	v.	explain it in an exact and detailed way 详细说明
element	[ˈɛləmənt]	n.	an abstract part of something 成分,要素
omit	[əˈmɪt]	v.	leave undone or leave out 省略
overall	[ˈoʊvɚˌɔːl]	a.	including everything 全部的,整体的

| limb | [lɪm] | n. | one of the jointed appendages of an animal used for locomotion or grasping: arm; leg; wing; flipper 肢 |
| superficial | [ˌsupɚˈfɪʃl] | a. | being or affecting or concerned with a surface; not deep or penetrating emotionally or intellectually 表面的, 肤浅的 |

Phrases & Expressions

from thence	following that 从此
leave off	to stop doing sth. 中断, 停止
be content with	happy and satisfied with what you have 满足于
aside from	except for 除……以外
in addition to	used when you want to menion another person or thing after sth. else 除……以外

1. This article is adapted from the book *The Language Instinct* by Steven Pinker (Sept. 18 1954—) an American Scientist, psychologist, linguist and author.

2. Shinar: The name Shinar occurs eight times in the Hebrew Bible, in which it refers to Babylonia. This location of Shinar is evident from its description as encompassing both Babel (Babylon) (in northern Babylonia) and Erech (Uruk) (in southern Babylonia).

3. Genesis: *Book of Genesis*, the first book of the Jewish Torah and the Christian Bible.

4. Martin Joos (1907—1978) was a linguist and German professor. He spent most of his career at the University of Wisconsin—Madison, and also served at the University of Toronto and as a visiting scholar at the University of Alberta, the University of Belgrade, and the University of Edinburgh. During World War II Joos was a cryptologist for the US Signal Security Agency. The War Department honored him with a Distinguished Service citation in recognition of his work developing communication systems. After the war he returned to the University of Wisconsin, eventually serving as the chairman of the Department of German. Among Joos's books on linguistics is *The Five Clocks* (1962), which introduced influential discussions of style, register and style-shifting.

5. Chomsky: Avram Noam Chomsky (December 7, 1928—)is an American linguist, philosopher, cognitive scientist, logician, political commentator, social justice activist, and anarcho-syndicalist advocate. Sometimes described as the "father of modern linguistics", Chomsky is also a major figure in analytic philosophy. He has spent most of his career at the Massachusetts Institute of Technology (MIT), where he is currently Professor Emeritus, and has authored over 100 books. He has been described as a prominent cultural figure, and was voted the "world's

top public intellectual" in a 2005 poll.

6. Noah: In Abrahamic religions, Noah or Noé or Noach was the tenth and last of the pre-flood Patriarchs. The story of Noah's Ark is told in the Torah in the Genesis flood narrative.

Task 1   Summarizing

Directions: Fill in the blanks in the following text outline with key points based on an overall understanding and then make an oral summary.

I. People left off the building of Babel because _____.

II. The conclusion of Martin Joos and Chomsky

    a. Martin Joos concluded that _____.

    b. According to Chomsky, _____.

III. Several most conspicuous ways in which languages can differ from what we are used to in English:

    a. English is a/an _____ language.

    b. English is a/an _____ language.

    c. English is a/an _____ language.

    d. English is a/an _____ language.

    e. English is a/an _____ language.

    f. In English, a noun can _____.

IV. Universal Grammar resembles _____.

Task 2   Reflecting on the Text

Directions: You have read the passage of the "the Tower of Babel." Discuss the following questions with your partner and then give an oral presentation of your reflections on the passage. You may organize your presentation by linking up your answers to the following questions.

Guiding Questions

1. According to the first sentence in Para. 1, how many languages did exist at that time?
2. Why did the Lord confound their language?
3. What is the conclusion of the linguist Martin Joos and when did the Chomskyan revolution begin?
4. What are the most conspicuous ways in which languages can differ from what we are used to in English?
5. According to the author, what are the similarities between Universal Grammar and an archetypal body plan?

Task 3   Making a Presentation

Directions: Give an oral presentation of your views on the following topics centering on "Whether the Whole World Should Speak a Single Language or Not." You should state your view clearly in the beginning, and then use your discussion results and other sources to support your points.

1. Give your clear stand (pros or cons) on the topic.
2. Give detailed arguments to support your stand.

Below are some words and expressions that you might find useful in your presentation.

1) Babel
2) Esperanto
3) cultural diversity
4) Łazarz Ludwik Zamenhof
5) cultural clash
6) globalization
7) universal language
8) misunderstanding
9) cross-culture communication
10) borderless

Part Four Cross Cultural Communication

Passage A

我的童年
莫言

  我小学未毕业即辍学,因为年幼体弱,干不了重活,只好到荒草滩上去放牧牛羊。当我牵着牛羊从学校门前路过,看到昔日的同学在校园里打打闹闹,我心中充满悲凉,深深地体会到一个人,哪怕是一个孩子,离开群体后的痛苦。

  到了荒滩上,我把牛羊放开,让它们自己吃草。蓝天如海,草地一望无际,周围看不到一个人影,没有人的声音,只有鸟儿在天上鸣叫。我感到很孤独,很寂寞,心里空空荡荡。有时候,我躺在草地上,望着天上懒洋洋地飘动着的白云,脑海里便浮现出许多莫名其妙的幻象。我们那地方流传着许多狐狸变成美女的故事,我幻想着能有一个狐狸变成美女与我来作伴放牛,但她始终没有出现。但有一次,一只火红色的狐狸从我面前的草丛中跳出来时,我被吓得一屁股蹲在地上。狐狸跑没了踪影,我还在那里颤抖。有时候我会蹲在牛的身旁,看着湛蓝的牛眼和牛眼中的我的倒影。有时候我会模仿着鸟儿的叫声试图与天上的鸟儿对话,有时候我会对一棵树诉说心声。但鸟儿不理我,树也不理我。许多年后,当我成为一个小说家,当年的许多幻想,都被我写进了小说。很多人夸我想象力丰富,有一些文学爱好者,希望我能告诉他们培养想象力的秘诀,对此,我只能报以苦笑。

  就像中国的先贤老子所说的那样:"福兮祸之所伏,祸兮福之所倚",我童年辍学,饱受饥饿、孤独、无书可读之苦,但我因此也像我们的前辈作家沈从文那样,及早地开始阅读社会人生这本大书。前面所提到的到集市上去听说书人说书,仅仅是这本大书中的一页。

  辍学之后,我混迹于成人之中,开始了"用耳朵阅读"的漫长生涯。二百多年前,我的故乡曾出了一个讲故事的伟大天才——蒲松龄,我们村里的许多人,包括我,都是他的传人。我在集体劳动的田间地头,在生产队的牛棚马厩,在我爷爷奶奶的热炕头上,甚至在摇摇晃晃地进行着的牛车社,聆听了许许多多神鬼故事,历史传奇,逸闻趣事,这些故事都与当地的自然环境,家庭历史紧密联系在一起,使我产生了强烈的现实感。

  我做梦也想不到有朝一日这些东西会成为我的写作素材,我当时只是一个迷恋故事的孩子,醉心地聆听着人们的讲述。那时我是一个绝对的有神论者,我相信万物都有灵性。我见到一棵大树会肃然起敬,我看到一只鸟会感到它随时会变化成人,我遇到一个陌生人,也会怀疑他是一个动物变化而成。每当夜晚我从生产队的记工房回家时,无边的恐惧便包围了我,为了壮胆,我一边奔跑一边大

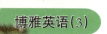

声歌唱。那时我正处在变声期，嗓音嘶哑，声调难听，我的歌唱，是对我的乡亲们的一种折磨。

1. 本篇节选自2012年诺贝尔文学奖获得者莫言的获奖感言。
2. 莫言，原名管谟业，1955年2月17日生，祖籍山东高密，中国当代著名作家。作品深受魔幻现实主义影响。2011年8月，莫言凭长篇小说《蛙》获第八届茅盾文学奖。2012年10月11日，莫言因其"用魔幻现实主义将民间故事、历史和现代融为一体"获得诺贝尔文学奖。

Word Bank

老子	(Taoist master) Laozi	福	fortune
祸	misfortune	说书人	storyteller
集体劳动	collective work/labor	热炕	heated kang
有神论者	theist	生产队	production team
记工	work points tallied	变声期	mutation

Directions: Please summarize the passage in English. Your summary should be about 150—200 words.

Passage B

The Dignity of Life and Death
Albert Camus

In receiving the distinction with which your free Academy has so generously honored me, my gratitude has be profound, particularly when I consider the extent to which this recompense has surpassed my personal merits. Every man, and for stronger reason, every artist, wants to be recognized. So do I. But I have not been able to learn of your decision without comparing its repercussions to what I really am. A man almost young, rich only in his doubts and with his work still in progress, accustomed to living in the solitude of work or in the retreats of friendship: how would he not feel a kind of panic at hearing the decree that transports him all of a sudden, alone and reduced to himself, to the centre of a glaring light? And with what feeling he could accept this honor at a time when other writers in Europe, among them the very greatest, are condemned to silence, and even at a time when the country of his birth is going through unending misery?

I felt that shock and inner turmoil. In order to regain peace I have had, in short, to come to terms with a too generous fortune. And since I cannot live up to it by merely resting on my achievement, I have found nothing to support me but what has supported me through all my life, even in the most contrary circumstances: the idea that I have of my art and of the role of the writer. Let me only tell you, in a spirit of gratitude and friendship, as simply as I can, what this idea is.

For myself, I cannot live without my art. But I have never placed it above everything. If, on the other hand, I need it, it is because it cannot be separated from my fellow men, and it allows me to live, such as I am, on one level with them. It is a means of stirring the greatest number of people by offering them a privileged picture of common joys and sufferings. It obliges the artist not to keep himself apart: it suggests him to the most humble and the most universal truth. And often he who has chosen the fate of the artist because he felt himself to be different soon realizes that he can maintain neither his art nor his difference unless he admits that he is like the others. The artist forges himself to the others, midway between the beauty he cannot do without and the community he cannot tear himself away from. That is why true artists scorn nothing: they are obliged to understand rather than to judge. And if they have to take sides in this world, they can perhaps side only with that society in which, according to Nietzsche's great words, not the judge but the creator will rule, whether he be a worker or an intellectual.

By the same token, the writer's role is not free from difficult duties. By definition he cannot put himself today in the service of those who make history: he is at the service of those who suffer it. Otherwise, he will be alone and deprived of his art. Not all the armies of tyranny with their millions of men will free him from his isolation, even and particularly if he falls into step with them. But the silence of an unknown prisoner, abandoned to humiliations at the other end of the world, is enough to draw the writer out of his exile, at least whenever, in the midst of the privileges of freedom, he manages not to forget that silence, and to transmit it in order to make it resound by means of his art.

None of us is great enough for such a task. But in all circumstances of life, in obscurity or temporary fame, cast in the irons of tyranny or for a time free to express himself, the writer can win the heart of a living community that will justify him, on the one condition that he will accept to the limit of his abilities the two tasks that constitute the greatest of his craft: the service of truth and the service of liberty. Because his task is to unite the greatest possible number of people, his art must not compromise with lies and servitude which, wherever they rule, breed solitude. Whatever our personal weaknesses may be, the nobility of our craft will always be rooted in two commitments, difficult to maintain: the refusal to lie about what one knows and the resistance to oppression.

For more than twenty years of an insane history, hopelessly lost like all the men of my generation in the convulsions of time, I have been supported by one thing: by the hidden feeling that to write today was an honor because this activity was a commitment—and a commitment not only to write. Specifically, in view of my powers and my state of being, it was a commitment to bear, together with all those who were living through the history, the misery and the hope we shared. These men, who were born at the beginning of the First World War, who were twenty when Hitler came to power and the first revolutionary trials were beginning, who were then confronted as a completion of their education with the Spanish Civil War, the Second World War, the world of concentration camps, a Europe of torture and prisons—these men must today rear their sons and create their works in a world threatened by nuclear destruction. Nobody, I think, can ask them to be optimists. And I even think that we should understand—without ceasing to fight it—the error of those who in an excess of despair have asserted their right to dishonour and have rushed into the nihilism of the era. But the fact remains that most of us, in my country and in Europe, have refused this nihilism and have engaged upon a quest for legitimacy. They have had to forge for themselves an art of living in times of catastrophe in order to be born a second time and to fight openly against the instinct of death at work in our history.

1. The passage was excerpted from the Nobel Prize acceptance speech by French writer Albert Camus in 1957 as the Nobel Prize winner for Literature.
2. Albert Camus [albɛʁ kamy] (November 7, 1913—January 4, 1960) was a French Nobel Prize winning author, journalist, and philosopher. His views contributed to the rise of the philosophy known as absurdism. He wrote in his essay "The Rebel" that his whole life was devoted to opposing the philosophy of nihilism while still delving deeply into individual freedom. Camus was awarded the 1957 Nobel Prize for Literature for "his important literary production, which with clear-sighted earnestness illuminates the problems of the human conscience in our times."

Directions: Please summarize the passage in Chinese. Your summary should be about 200—300 words.

Unit 2

HISTORY AND CIVILIZATION

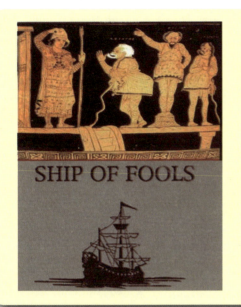

The story of Greek life is a story not only of moderation but also of simplicity.

—*From Greek Life by Hendrik van Loon*

Fashion favored the composition of these ships, whose crew of imaginary heroes, ethical models, or social types embarked on a great symbolic voyage which would bring them, if not fortune, then at least the figure of their destiny or their truth.

—*From Madness and Civilization by Michel Foucault*

Learning Objectives

Upon the completion of this unit, you should be able to

Remembering & Understanding	★ read Text A and Text B aloud smoothly with expression indicative of comprehension and tone; ★ identify and explain in your own words the thesis and the major points of Text A and Text B;
Analyzing & Applying	★ make reference to comparison sentences of Text A in your writing; ★ produce adverbial clauses of concession with however and whenever; ★ use definition and definition expanding methods for definition essay writing;
Evaluating & Creating	★ incorporate description, exemplification, and etc. in definition paragraph; ★ deliver a clear and coherent oral presentation of your views on the ship of fools and social injustice.

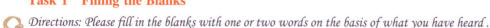

Part One Lead-in

Section 1 Listening: American Indians

Task 1 Filling the Blanks

Directions: Please fill in the blanks with one or two words on the basis of what you have heard.

November is National American Indian and Alaska Native Heritage month in the United States. It _____ the history, culture and _____ of American Indians and Alaska Native people. So, this week, we answer two listener questions about American Indians. Godswill Eke Kalu from Nigeria asks why Native Americans are called Indians. And Amrit Rai from Nepal asks about the _____ situation of American Indians today.

The European _____ Christopher Columbus gave the name "Indians" to the native peoples of North and South America. He thought that he had reached a place called the Indies. In time, the terms "American Indian" and "Indian" became widely used.

The United States Bureau of Indian Affairs says the term "Native American" started to be used in the 1960s. It _____ American Indians and Alaska Natives. Later the term also included Native Hawaiians and Pacific Islanders. The government _____ says the Eskimos and Aleuts of Alaska do not like to be called "Indians". They call themselves "Alaska Natives."

Many American Indians _____ the term "Native American." They say it tries to describe too many different groups of people, including American Samoans, Aleuts and Hawaiians. These people want to be called "American Indians." Some want to be known by their tribe, such as Lakota or Navajo.

The United States Census Bureau says more than four million American Indians and Alaska natives lived in the country in 2004. Some live on government land called reservations or tribal lands. Others live in cities and towns.

The economic situation of American Indians as a group is not good. A continuing study by Harvard University says that American Indians _____ earn less money than other Americans. It also says that they have more _____, higher rates of death and disease and less family unity than other American groups.

However, the study is also finding that an increasing number of tribes are creating successful business. For example, the Pequot tribe in the northeast owns and _____ a hotel, gambling casino and museum of its culture and history. You can learn about a famous chief of the Lakota Indians known as Crazy Horse next time.

Task 2 Group Discussion

Directions: Please discuss the following questions in pairs or groups based on what you have heard.

1. According to the audio clip, who gave the name "Indians" to the native peoples of North and South America?
2. When did the term "Native American" begin to be used?

3. How is the economic situation of American Indians today?

Section 2 Watching: Civilization in the West History

Task 1 Group Discussion

Directions: Please watch the video clip "Civilization in the West History" and discuss the three questions below in pairs or groups.

1. Why should Vasco da Gama sail to find a new shipping route?
2. When did Vasco da Gama start his journey?
3. What are the differences between Vasco da Gama's and Zheng He's sail?

Task 2 Imitation

Directions: Please watch the video again, and try to imitate the speaker's pronunciation and intonation.

Size isn't everything. Admiral Zheng He's enormous ships and his emperor's grandiose ambitions had done precious little for China. How very different it would be for the altogether more modest voyages about to be undertaken by a remarkable man from the tiny European kingdom of Portugal. His name was Vasco da Gama. Da Gama made his country's-and his own-fortune by cornering the market in the 15th century's favourite food additive, spices.

Part Two Reading and Writing

Text A

Greek Life—How The Greeks Lived
Hendrik van Loon

1   In all matters of government, the Greek *democracy* recognised only one class of *citizens* the freemen. Every Greek city was *composed* of a small number of free born citizens, a large number of slaves and a *sprinkling* of foreigners.

2   *At rare intervals* (usually during a war, when men were needed for the army) the Greeks showed themselves willing to confer the rights of citizenship upon the "barbarians" as they called the foreigners. But this was an *exception*. Citizenship was a matter of birth. You were an *Athenian* because your father and your grandfather had been Athenians before you. But however great your *merits* as a trader or a soldier, if you were born of non-Athenian parents, you remained a "foreigner" until the end of time.

3   The Greek city, therefore, whenever it was not ruled by a king or a tyrant, was run by and for the freemen, and this would not have been possible without a large army of slaves who outnumbered the free citizens at the rate of six or five to one and who

performed those tasks to which we modern people must devote most of our time and energy if we wish to provide for our families and pay the rent of our apartments. The slaves did all the cooking and baking and candlestick making of the entire city. They were the tailors and the *carpenters* and the jewelers and the school-teachers and the bookkeepers and they *tended* the store and looked after the factory while the master went to the public meeting to discuss questions of war and peace or visited the theatre to see the latest play of *Aeschylus* or hear a discussion of the *revolutionary* ideas of *Euripides*, who had dared to express certain doubts upon the omnipotence of the great god Zeus.

4 Indeed, ancient Athens *resembled* a modern club. All the freeborn citizens were *hereditary* members and all the slaves were hereditary servants, and waited upon the needs of their masters, and it was very pleasant to be a member of the organisation.

5 But when we talk about slaves. We do not mean the sort of people about whom you have read in the pages of "*Uncle Tom's Cabin*." It is true that the position of those slaves who *tilled* the fields was a very unpleasant one, but the average freeman who had come down in the world and who had been obliged to hire himself out as a farm hand led just as *miserable* a life. In the cities, furthermore, many of the slaves were more prosperous than the poorer classes of the freemen. For the Greeks, who loved moderation in all things, did not like to treat their slaves after the fashion which afterward was so common in Rome, where a slave had as few rights as an engine in a modern factory and could be thrown to the wild animals upon the smallest pretext.

6 The Greeks accepted slavery as a necessary institution, without which no city could possibly become the home of a truly *civilised* people.

7 The slaves also took care of those tasks which nowadays are performed by the business men and the professional men. As for those *household* duties which *take up* so much of the time of your mother and which worry your father when he comes home from his office, the Greeks, who understood the value of leisure, had reduced such duties to the smallest possible *minimum* by living amidst surroundings of extreme *simplicity*.

8 To begin with, their homes were very plain. Even the rich nobles spent their lives in a sort of adobe barn, which lacked all the comforts which a modern workman expects as his natural right. A Greek home consisted of four walls and a roof. There was a door which led into the street but there were no windows. The kitchen, the living rooms and the sleeping *quarters* were built around an open courtyard in which there was a small fountain, or a statue and a few plants to make it look bright. Within this courtyard the family lived when it did not rain or when it was not too cold. In one corner of the yard the cook (who was a slave) prepared the meal and in another corner, the teacher (who was also a slave) taught the children the *alpha beta gamma* and *the tables of multiplication* and in still another corner the lady of the house, who rarely left her domain (since it was not considered good form for a married woman to be seen on the street too often) was repairing her husband's coat with her seamstresses (who

were slaves), and in the little office, right off the door, the master was inspecting the accounts which the overseer of his farm (who was a slave) had just brought to him.

9   When dinner was ready the family came together but the meal was a very simple one and did not take much time. The Greeks seem to have regarded eating as an *unavoidable* evil and not a *pastime*, which kills many dreary hours and eventually kills many dreary people. They lived on bread and on wine, with a little meat and some green vegetables. They drank water only when nothing else was available because they did not think it very healthy. They loved to call on each other for dinner, but our idea of a festive meal, where everybody is supposed to eat much more than is good for him, would have disgusted them. They came together at the table for the purpose of a good talk and a good glass of wine and water, but as they were moderate people they *despised* those who drank too much.

10   The same simplicity which *prevailed* in the dining room also dominated their choice of clothes. They liked to be clean and well groomed, to have their hair and beards neatly cut, to feel their bodies strong with the exercise and the swimming of the gymnasium, but they never followed the Asiatic fashion which *prescribed* loud colours and strange patterns. They wore a long white coat and they managed to look as smart as a modern Italian officer in his long blue cape.

11   They loved to see their wives wear *ornaments* but they thought it very vulgar to display their wealth (or their wives) in public and whenever the women left their home they were as inconspicuous as possible.

12   In short, the story of Greek life is a story not only of moderation but also of simplicity. "Things," chairs and tables and books and houses and carriages, are *apt to* take up a great deal of their owner's time. In the end they invariably make him their slave and his hours are spent looking after their wants, keeping them polished and brushed and painted. The Greeks, before everything else, wanted to be "free," both in mind and in body. That they might maintain their liberty, and be truly free in spirit, they reduced their daily needs to the lowest possible point.

New Words

democracy	[dɪˈmɑːkrəsi]	n.	a system of government in which people choose their rulers by voting for them in elections 民主;民主制度
citizen	[ˈsɪtɪzn]	n.	a native or naturalized member of a state or other political community 公民;市民
compose	[kəmˈpəʊz]	v.	to form the substance of 组成,构成
sprinkling	[ˈsprɪŋklɪŋ]	n.	a small number 少量,一点儿
exception	[ɪkˈsɛpʃən]	n.	an instance that does not conform to a rule or generalization 例外,除外
Athenian	[əˈθiːnɪən]	n.	a resident of Athens 雅典人

merit	[ˈmɛrɪt]	n.	any admirable quality or attribute 价值,优点
carpenter	[ˈkɑːpəntə(r)]	n.	a woodworker who makes or repairs wooden objects 木工,木匠
tend	[tɛnd]	v.	to take care of or look after 照料,照管
revolutionary	[ˌrɛvəˈluːʃəneri]	a.	markedly new or introducing radical change 革命的；革命性的,创新的
resemble	[rɪˈzɛmbəl]	v.	appear like; be similar or bear a likeness to 与……相像,类似于
hereditary	[həˈrɛdɪteri]	a.	tending to occur among members of a family usually by heredity 遗传的,世袭的；遗传性
till	[tɪl]	v.	work land as by ploughing, harrowing, and manuring, in order to make it ready for cultivation 耕种,耕作
miserable	[ˈmɪzrəbl]	a.	very unhappy; full of misery 悲惨的；痛苦的
civilised	[ˈsɪvəˌlaɪzd]	a.	having a high state of culture and development both social and technological 文明的；非野蛮的；有礼貌的；有教养的
household	[ˈhaʊshold]	a.	relating to family house 家庭的
minimum	[ˈmɪnəməm]	n.	the smallest possible quantity 最低限度；最小量
simplicity	[sɪmˈplɪsɪti]	n.	the quality of being simple or uncompounded 简单,朴素；质朴
quarter	[ˈkwɔːtə(r)]	n.	a district of a city having some distinguishing character 地区
unavoidable	[ˌʌnəˈvɔɪdəbəl]	a.	impossible to avoid or evade 不可避免的
pastime	[ˈpæstaɪm]	n.	something that you do in your spare time because you enjoy it or are interested in it 消遣,娱乐
despise	[dɪˈspaɪz]	v.	look down on with disdain 鄙视,看不起
prevail	[prɪˈveɪl]	v.	be larger in number, quantity, power, status or importance 流行,盛行
prescribe	[prɪˈskraɪb]	v.	issue commands or orders for 指定,规定
ornament	[ˈɔːrnəmənt]	n.	an attractive object that you display at home, in the garden or similar places 装饰；装饰物

Phrases & Expressions

at intervals	with time between 不时,相隔一定距离
take up	to fill or use an amount of space or time 占据；占用
alpha beta gamma	the first three letters of the Greek alphabet, referring to Greek language; 希腊语言头三个字母

the tables of multiplication	a list showing the results when a number is multiplied by a set of numbers, esp. 1 to 12, in turn 九九乘法表
be apt to	likely or having a natural tendency to do sth. 易于……,倾向于……

Notes

1. The article was selected from *"The Story of Mankind,"* written by Hendrik van Loon, first published in 1921. *The Story of Mankind* has charmed generations of readers of all ages with its warmth, simplicity and wisdom. Beginning with the origins of human life and sweeping forward to illuminate all of history, Hendrik van Loon's incomparable prose enlivens the characters and events of every age. His unique ability to convey history as a fascinating tale of adventure has endeared the book to countless readers and has accorded it a unique place in publishing history.
2. Aeschylus: Greek tragedian; the father of Greek tragic drama (525—456 BC). 希腊的悲剧作家埃斯库罗斯,希腊悲剧之父。
3. Euripides: one of the greatest tragic dramatists of ancient Greece (480—406 BC). 希腊的悲剧诗人欧里庇得斯。
4. *Uncle Tom's Cabin:* a life Among the Lowly, was an anti-slavery novel by American author Harriet Beecher Stowe (June 14, 1821—July 1, 1896), published in 1852.

Task 1 Generating the Outline

Directions: Please identify the thesis of the passage and the main point of each paragraph, and then find out how these points develop the thesis. You may use the table below for your help.

Para. 1: The introduction	Life in ancient Greece: Greek democracy recognized only _____. Every Greek city was composed of a small number of _____, a large number of _____ and a sprinkling of _____.
Para. 2: The definition	Citizenship is _____. If you were born of non-Athenian parents, you remained a _____.
Para. 3: The description	The Greek city was run by and for the _____ with a large army of _____ who did a lot of _____.
Para. 4: The analogy/ comparison	Ancient Athens resembled _____. All the freeborn citizens were _____ and all the slaves were _____.
Para. 5: The description	Slaves do not mean the sort of people about whom you have read in the pages of _____.
Para. 6: The description	Slavery was accepted as _____ by the Greeks.
Para. 7: The description	The slaves took care of those tasks which nowadays are performed by _____ and the _____ duties.

Para. 8: The description	Homes of Greeks were very _____.
Para. 9: The definition	Eating was regarded as an _____ and not a _____.
Para. 10: The definition	The simplicity _____ their choice of clothes.
Para. 11: The description	They did not love to display _____ in public.
Para. 12: The conclusion	The story of Greek life is a story not only of _____ but also of _____.

Task 2   Understanding the Text

Directions: Please answer the following ten questions based on text A.

1. According to the article, what are the compositions of the Greek city?
2. How did the Greeks get their citizenship?
3. How does the author summarize the structure of the Greek city?
4. What were the duties of the slaves?
5. What attitude did the Greeks hold to slavery?
6. What was the Greek home like?
7. What did the Greeks think about dinners or meals?
8. What did the Greeks like to dress?
9. How did the Greeks regard wealth?
10. How does the author summarize the Greek life?

Task 3   Vocabulary Building

Directions: One way to form an adjective is to add the suffix -ary to a noun or a verb.

revolution + ary → revolutionary   heredity + ary → hereditary

Study the following adjectives formed by adding -ary to nouns and complete the following sentences with them.

mission	+ ary	missionary
imagine	+ ary	imaginary
evolution	+ ary	evolutionary
budget	+ ary	budgetary
function	+ ary	functionary
prime	+ ary	primary

1. For _____ reasons, the redevelopment of these systems can be a poor option.
2. If we are derived from the same _____ process as all other living creatures, I'm not sure that this explanation has the appropriate explanatory power.
3. Our company has targeted career women as our _____ customers.
4. While not everyone has the _____ gift, every Christian is called to be on a mission to all four groups in some way.
5. Though all the characters in the books were _____, he liked them so much.
6. Mr. Smith says that he had some sort of _____ position in that organization.

Unit 2

Directions: The noun when added with the suffix -ship forms another noun indicating state quality, office, skill or condition.

citizen + ship → citizenship   friend + ship → friendship

Study the following nouns formed by adding -ship and complete the following sentences with them.

king	+ ship	kingship
governor	+ ship	governorship
student	+ ship	studentship
relation	+ ship	relationship
craftsman	+ ship	craftsmanship
apprentice	+ ship	apprenticeship

1. Their childhood and _____ both gave the impression of technology-oriented people.
2. Someone who has (a)n _____ works for a fixed period of time for a person who has a particular skill in order to learn the skill.
3. Traditions of _____ suggest that the succession line should pass through brothers of one generation in order of age, before descending to the next.
4. The artist's work shows the perfect union of _____ and imagination.
5. Richard Nixon "retired" in 1962 after losing an election for the _____ of California.
6. His _____ with Mary went through four stages.

Task 4 Learning the Phrases

Directions: Please fill in the blanks of the sentences below with the phrases listed in the box. Change the forms if necessary. Notice that some phrases need to be used more than once.

| be composed of | a sprinkling of | at rare intervals | apt to |
| amidst surroundings of | take up | upon the smallest pretext | |

1. We are _____ wish for what we can't have.
2. He did not particularly want to _____ a competitive sport.
3. I tackled him about how anyone could live _____ so much poverty.
4. Don't you have _____ common sense?
5. They would restart the war _____.
6. I know how busy you must be and naturally I wouldn't want to _____ too much of your time.
7. Beginners are too _____ make mistakes in grammar.
8. He didn't attend that meeting _____ of sickness.
9. The shop name shall _____ more than two Chinese characters.
10. He visits the town _____.

Task 5 Studying the Sentence Structure

Sentences with comparison

Sentences from the text

1. Indeed, ancient Athens resembled a modern club. (Para. 2)
2. All the freeborn citizens were hereditary members and all the slaves were hereditary servants, and waited upon the needs of their masters, and it was very pleasant to be a member of the organisation. (Para. 2)
3. For the Greeks, who loved moderation in all things, did not like to treat their slaves after the fashion which afterward was so common in Rome, where a slave had as few rights as an engine in a modern factory...(Para. 5)
4. They wore a long white coat and they managed to look as smart as a modern Italian officer in his long blue cape. (Para. 10)

Directions: Please follow the examples and create five sentences with comparison on your own.
Tips

1. In writing, we can compare two different or similar things to make the explanation in more details.
2. To compare two different things is referred to as "contrast" and the opposition is called "comparison," which focuses on explaining how two things or more things are alike.
3. Useful expressions for similarity are as follows: resemble, be, like, similar to, also, similarly, in the same way, likewise, again, in like manner, in the same manner, equally, just as, and so on.

1. _____
2. _____
3. _____
4. _____
5. _____

Sentences of adverbial clauses of Concession by whenever/however...

Sentences from the text

1. But however great your merits as a trader or a soldier, if you were born of non-Athenian parents, you remained a "foreigner" until the end of time. (Para. 2)
2. The Greek city, therefore, whenever it was not ruled by a king or a tyrant, was run by and for the freemen. (Para. 2)
3. Whenever the women left their home they were as inconspicuous as possible. (Para. 11)

Directions: Please follow the examples and create five adverbial clauses of concession on your own.
Tips

1. "Whenever" can be used to lead both the time and concession clause. When it leads the concession clause, it means "at whatever time, no matter when." When it's used in time clause, it's similar to "when" with the meaning of "every time, the moment..., as soon as, once."

2. When "however" is used in the concession clause, it is followed by adjectives or adverbs: however+ adj./adv.+subject+(verb). It equals to "no matter how."

1. _____
2. _____
3. _____
4. _____
5. _____

Task 6 Paraphrasing Difficult Sentences

1. At rare intervals (usually during a war, when men were needed for the army) the Greeks showed themselves willing to confer the rights of citizenship upon the "barbarians" as they called the foreigners.

   _____
   _____.

2. The Greek city, therefore, whenever it was not ruled by a king or a tyrant, was run by and for the freemen, and this would not have been possible without a large army of slaves who outnumbered the free citizens at the rate of six or five to one and who performed those tasks to which we modern people must devote most of our time and energy if we wish to provide for our families and pay the rent of our apartments.

   _____
   _____.

3. They were the tailors and the carpenters and the jewelers and the school-teachers and the bookkeepers and they tended the store and looked after the factory while the master went to the public meeting to discuss questions of war and peace or visited the theatre to see the latest play of *Aeschylus* or hear a discussion of the revolutionary ideas of Euripides, who had dared to express certain doubts upon the omnipotence of the great god Zeus.

   _____
   _____.

4. As for those household duties which take up so much of the time of your mother and which worry your father when he comes home from his office, the Greeks, who understood the value of leisure, had reduced such duties to the smallest possible minimum by living amidst surroundings of extreme simplicity.

   _____
   _____.

5. They loved to see their wives wear ornaments but they thought it very vulgar to display their wealth (or their wives) in public and whenever the women left their home they were as inconspicuous as possible.

   _____
   _____.

Task 7 Summarizing the Text

Directions: Please summarize Text A in 100 words. You may use the table in Task 1 to help you.

Task 8 Writing with Definition

Directions: Write a passage of three paragraphs by using definition on the topic "Who or What is a hero". In the first paragraph, you should select a topic you personally feel needs more clarification. In the second paragraph, you should try to define that heroes have different definitions in the present society. When introducing different types of heroes, you need to give some specific definitions from different people and what heroes represent in the society. In the third paragraph, you need to summarize what heroes have in common. Your writing should be about 200 words. You may use what is provided below in the box for your help.

Tips

1. A definition tells what a term means and how it differs from other terms in its class. It's usually classified into two groups: formal definition and extended definitions. The former gives brief, succinct explanations; while another with longer and more complex definition requires a paragraph, an essay, or even a whole book to explain what something, or even someone is.

2. Definitions could be expanded with five different patterns of development as follows: Exemplification (giving examples); Description; Comparison and Contrast; Process; Classification and Division.

3. In addition to using various patterns of development, the following strategies can be used to expand the body of definition. You can define a term by using Synonyms (words with similar meanings), Negation (telling what it is not), Enumeration (listing its characteristics), Analogies (comparisons identifying similarities between the term and something dissimilar), and Origin and Development (the word's derivation, original meaning and usages).

> Referring to what a hero is, the first thing that flashes to my mind is always a man who [...]
> As far as I'm concerned, different people have different judging standards on heroes. [...]
> However, it can't be denied that all heroes have some personalities in common, which [...]

Part Three   Reading and Speaking

Text B

Madness and Civilization
Michel Foucault

1   Something new appears in the *imaginary* landscape of the *Renaissance*; soon it will occupy a privileged place there: the Ship of Fools, a strange "drunken boat" that *glides* along the calm rivers of the Rhineland and the Flemish canals.

2   The Narrenschyff, of course, is a literary composition, probably borrowed from the old *Argonaut* cycle, one of the great mythic themes recently *revived* and rejuvenated, acquiring an institutional aspect in the Burgundy Estates. Fashion favored the composition of these Ships, whose crew of imaginary heroes, ethical models, or social types *embarked on* a great symbolic voyage which would bring them, if not fortune, then at least the figure of their destiny or their truth. Thus Symphorien Champier composes *a Ship of Princes and Battles of Nobility* in 1502, then *a Ship of Virtuous Ladies* in 1503; there is also *a Ship of Health*, alongside the Blauive Schute of Jacob van Oestvoren in 1413, Sebastian Brant's *Narrenschiff* (1494), and the work of Josse Bade-Stultiferae naviculae scaphae fatuarum mulierum (1498). Bosch's painting, of course, *belongs to* this dream *fleet*.

3   But of all these romantic or satiric *vessels*, the Narrenschiff is the only one that had a real existence—for they did exist, these boats that *conveyed* their *insane cargo* from town to town. Madmen then led an easy wandering existence. The towns drove them outside their limits; they were allowed to wander in the open countryside, when not entrusted to a group of *merchants* and pilgrims. The custom was especially frequent in Germany; in Nuremberg, in the first half of the fifteenth century, the presence of 63 madmen had been registered; 31 were driven away; in the fifty years that followed, there are records of 21 more obligatory departures; and these are only the madmen arrested by the municipal *authorities*. Frequently they were handed over to boatmen: in Frankfort, in 1399, seamen were *instructed* to rid the city of a madman who walked about the streets *naked*; in the first years of the fifteenth century, a criminal madman was expelled in the same manner from Mainz. Sometimes the sailors disembarked these bothersome passengers sooner than they had promised; *witness* a blacksmith of Frankfort twice expelled and twice returning before being taken to Kreuznach for good. Often the cities of Europe must have seen these "ships of fools" approaching their harbors.

4   It is not easy to discover the exact meaning of this custom. One might suppose it was a general means of extradition（引渡）by which municipalities sent wandering madmen out of their own jurisdiction; a hypothesis which will not in itself *account for* the facts, since certain madmen, even before special houses were built for them, were admitted to hospitals and cared for as such; at the Hotel-Dieu in Paris, their cots（小床）were set up in the dormitories. Moreover, in the majority of the cities of Europe there existed throughout the Middle Ages and the Renaissance a place of detention *reserved* for the insane; there was for example the Chatelet of Melun or the famous Tour aux Fous in Caen; there were the numberless Narrtunner of Germany, like the gates of Lubeck or the Jungpfer of Hamburg. Madmen were thus not invariably expelled. One might then speculate that among them only foreigners were driven away, each city agreeing to care for those madmen among its own citizens. Do we not in fact find among the account books of certain medieval cities subsidies for madmen or donations made for the care of the insane? However, the problem is not so simple,

for there existed gathering places where the madmen, more numerous than elsewhere, were not autoch-thonous(土生的). First come the shrines: Saint-Mathurin de Larchant, Saint-Hildevert de Gournay, Besancon, Gheel; pilgrimages to these places were organized, often supported, by cities or hospitals. It is possible that these ships of fools, which haunted the imagination of the entire early Renaissance, were pilgrimage boats, highly symbolic cargoes of madmen *in search of* their reason: some went down the Rhineland rivers toward Belgium and Gheel; others sailed up the Rhine toward the Jura and Besancon.

5 What matters is that the vagabond madmen, the act of driving them away, their departure and embarkation do not assume their entire significance on the plane of social *utility* or *security*. Other meanings much closer to *rite* are certainly present; and we can still discern some traces of them. Thus *access to* churches was denied to madmen, although ecclesiastical(基督教的) law did not deny them the use of the sacraments(圣事). The Church takes no action against a priest who goes mad; but in Nuremberg in 1421 a mad priest was expelled with particular solemnity, as if the impurity was *multiplied* by the *sacred* nature of his person, and the city put on its budget the money given him as a viaticum(旅费). It happened that certain madmen were publicly *whipped*, and in the course of kind of a game they were *chased* in a mock race and driven out of the city with quarterstaff(铁头木棒) *blows*. So many signs that the expulsion of madmen had become one of a number of *ritual* exiles.

6 Thus we better understand the curious implication assigned to the *navigation* of madmen and the prestige attending it. On the one hand, we must not minimize its incontestable practical effectiveness: to hand a madman over to sailors was to be *permanently* sure he would not be prowling(徘徊) beneath the city walls; it made sure that he would go far away; it made him a prisoner of his own departure. But water adds to this the dark mass of its own values; it carries off, but it does more: it purifies. Navigation delivers man to the uncertainty of fate; on water, each of us is in the hands of his own destiny; every embarkation is, potentially, the last. It is for the other world that the madman sets sail in his fools' boat; it is from the other world that he comes when he disembarks. The madman's voyage is at once a rigorous division and an absolute passage. In one sense, it simply develops, across a half-real, half-imaginary geography, the madman's luminal(最低量) position on the horizon of medieval concern—a position symbolized and made real at the same time by the madman's privilege of being *confined* within the city gates: his exclusion must enclose him; if he cannot and must not have another prison than the threshold itself, he is kept at the point of passage. He is put in the interior of the exterior, and inversely. A highly symbolic position, which will doubtless remain his until our own day, if we are willing to admit that what was formerly a visible *fortress* of order has now become the castle of our *conscience*.

Unit 2

New Words

imaginary	[ɪˈmædʒɪnɛri]	a.	existing only in your mind or in a story, and not in real life 虚构的,想象的
renaissance	[ˈrenəsɑːns]	n.	the period in Europe, especially Italy, in the 14th, 15th, and 16th centuries, when there was a new interest in art, literature, science, and learning 文艺复兴
glide	[glaɪd]	v.	to move silently and in a smooth and effortless way 滑行
argonaut	[ˈɑrgəˌnɔt]	n.	someone engaged in a dangerous but potentially rewarding adventure <希神>亚尔古英雄(随同贾森乘亚尔古舟,去海外寻找金羊毛的英雄)
revive	[rɪˈvaɪv]	v.	give new life or energy to 复活,恢复
fleet	[flit]	n.	a group of ships organized to do something together, for example, to fight battles or to catch fish 舰队;船队
vessel	[ˈvɛsl]	n.	a ship or large boat 船;舰
convey	[kənˈve]	v.	to transfer to another 运送;传送
insane	[ɪnˈsen]	a.	very foolish; afflicted with or characteristic of mental derangement 疯狂的;精神病的
cargo	[ˈkɑrgo]	n.	the goods that a ship or plane is carrying 货物
merchant	[ˈmɝtʃənt]	n.	a person who buys or sells goods in large quantities, especially one who imports and exports them 商人
authority	[əˈθɔrəti]	n.	an official organization or government department that has the power to make decisions 当局
instruct	[ɪnˈstrʌkt]	v.	to give instructions or directions for some task 命令;指导
naked	[ˈnekɪd]	a.	completely unclothed 裸体的
witness	[ˈwɪtnəs]	v.	to see something happen 目击
reserve	[rɪˈzɝv]	v.	to obtain or arrange (for oneself) in advance 储备,预定
utility	[juˈtɪləti]	n.	the quality of being of practical use 实用
security	[səˈkjʊrəti]	n.	a condition of being safe and free from worry 安全

rite	[raɪt]	n.	a traditional ceremony that is carried out by a particular group or within a particular society 仪式,礼仪
multiply	[ˈmʌltɪplaɪ]	v.	increase greatly in number or amount 大大增加
sacred	[ˈsekrɪd]	a.	holy, connected with religion or used in religious ceremonies 神圣的;庄严的,宗教的
whip	[wɪp]	v.	to beat severely with a whip or rod 鞭打;抽打
chase	[tʃeɪs]	v.	to run after someone or follow someone quickly in order to catch or reach them 追赶
blow	[blo]	n.	a hit with a fist or weapon 打击;殴打
ritual	[ˈrɪtʃuəl]	a.	of or relating to or characteristic of religious rites 作为仪式的一部分的;礼节性的
navigation	[ˌnævəˈgeʃən]	n.	deciding the movement of a ship or an aircraft, which course to follow 导航;航海
permanently	[ˈpɚmənəntli]	ad.	lasting forever 永久地
confine	[kənˈfaɪn]	v.	to prevent something from spreading beyond a place or group 将(某事物)控制(在某地范围内)
fortress	[ˈfɔːrtrəs]	n.	a castle or other large strong building, or a well-protected place, which is intended to be difficult for enemies to enter 堡垒,要塞
conscience	[ˈkɑːnʃəns]	n.	the part of your mind that tells you whether what you are doing is right or wrong 良心;道德心

Phrases & Expressions

embark on	to start to do sth. new or difficult 着手,开始做某事
belong to	to be part of a particular group, type or system 属于
account for	to give an explanation of sth. 解释;说明
in search of	looking for 寻找
access to	to reach, enter or use sth. 进入

1. This passage was adapted from "Madness and Civilization" by Michel Foucault. Madness and Civilization is a 1964 abridged edition of French philosopher Michel Foucault's 1961 work Folie et Déraison: Histoire de la folie à l'âge classique. An English translation of the complete 1961 edition, entitled *History of Madness*, was published in June 2006. Foucault's first major book, it is an examination of the evolving meaning of madness in European

culture, law, politics, philosophy and medicine from the Middle Ages to the end of the eighteenth century, and a critique of historical method and the idea of history. It marks a turning in Foucault's thought away from phenomenology toward structuralism: though he uses the language of phenomenology to describe an evolving experience of "the other" as mad, he attributes this evolution to the influence of specific powerful social structures.

2. Ship of Fools: It is an allegory, originating from Plato, which has long been a fixture in Western literature and art. The allegory depicts a vessel populated by human inhabitants who are deranged, frivolous, or oblivious passengers aboard a ship without a pilot, and seemingly ignorant of their own direction. This concept makes up the framework of the 15th century book *Das Narrenschyff and Narragoniam* (1494) by Sebastian Brant. This book may have served as the inspiration for Hieronymous Bosch's famous painting, Ship of Fools: a ship—an entire fleet at first—sets off from Basel to the paradise of fools. In literary and artistic compositions of the 15th and 16th centuries, the cultural motif of the ship of fools also served to parody the "ark of salvation" as the Catholic Church was styled.

3. Das Narrenschyff: modern German for *Ship of Fools*

4. Symphorien Champier (1471—1538), a Lyonnese doctor born in Saint-Symphorien, France, was a relation of the Chevalier de Bayard through his wife, Marguerite Terrail.

5. Josse Bade (1462—1535) was a pioneer of the printing industry, and also a renowned grammarian and pedagogue. His work *Navicula Stultarum Mulierum*, a satire on the follies of women.

6. Sebastian Brant (1457—10 May, 1521) was a German humanist and satirist. He is best known for his satire *Das Narrenschyff* (*The Ship of Fools*).

7. Chatelet of Melun: one of the famous psychiatric hospital in Paris

8. Lubeck or the Jungpfer of Hamburg: a city in northwestern Germany and an important Baltic port; a leading member of the Hanseatic League.

Task 1   Summarizing

Directions: Fill in the blanks in the following text outline with key points based on an overall understanding and then make an oral summary.

I. Something new appears: _____.

II. What's Narrenschyff?
   a. Narrenschyff is borrowed from _____.
   b. Narrenschyff is the only one _____.

III. Reasons for the existence of Narrenschyff:
   a. One might suppose _____.
   b. One might then speculate that _____.
   c. It's possible that these ships of fools _____.
   d. Other meanings much closer to _____.

IV. Implications assigned to the navigation of madmen:
   a. We must not minimize its incontestable practical effectiveness: _____.
   b. But water adds to this the dark mass of its own values: _____.

Task 2　Reflecting on the Text

Directions: You have read the story of the "ship of fools". Discuss the following questions with your partner and then give an oral presentation of your reflections on the story. You may organize your presentation by linking up your answers to the questions below.

Guiding Questions:
1. What's the new phenomenon in the imaginary landscape of the Renaissance?
2. What's the meaning of Narrenschyff?
3. Are there any novels influenced by the ship of fools?
4. What's the function of the ship of fools?
5. What did the people usually do with the insane? Why did they do so?
6. Could the madmen get access to the church?
7. What's the possible meaning of the madman's voyage according to the author?
8. How do you reflect on the action of driving any madmen onto the ship of fools?
9. How do you reflect on the social status of the madmen at that time?
10. What's the implication of the passage?

Task 3　Making a Presentation

Directions: Give an oral presentation of your views on the following topics centering on "Ship of Fools and Social Injustice." You should state your view clearly in the beginning, and then use your discussion results and other sources to support your points.

1. Introduce the ship of fools with several sentences.
2. Relate the treatment on madmen in the story to the social injustice.

Below are some words and expressions that you might find useful in your presentation.

1) harmonious development	2) civilized society
3) equality	4) core value
5) justice	6) the differences in treatment
7) normal persons	8) moral ethics
9) uncertainty of fate	10) prejudice

Part Four　Cross Cultural Communication

Passage A

郑和下西洋——三保太监的不朽航程

　　15世纪初，一支浩浩荡荡的船队从南京起航。这次远航揭开了其后一连串海上航行的序幕，并在短暂时间内为中国确立了大国领先的地位。郑和统帅了这次远航，他是中国历史上最重要的探险家，也是举世闻名的最伟大的航海家之一。事实上，还有些人认为他是传说中水手辛巴达的原型。

Unit 2

　　公元1371年,郑和出生在现在的云南省的一个穆斯林家庭里。他的父母给他取名为马三保。马三保11岁时,被入侵云南的明军掳至南京,被净身后入宫,选去王府做内宫太监。

　　马三保在王府期间和皇太子成为了好朋友,皇太子后来成为明成祖永乐皇帝,是明代最出色的皇帝之一。马三保英勇、强壮、足智多谋,又赤胆忠心,因此深得皇太子的信赖。皇太子登基之后,赐给马三保"郑和"这个新的名字,同时提升他为内宫监太监。

　　永乐皇帝是个雄心勃勃的皇帝,他相信通过国际贸易及外交上的"门户开放"政策,中国会在世界上享有更高的声望。公元1405年,永乐皇帝下诏让中国船队远航到印度洋,并派遣郑和负责此趟航程。在以后的28年里,郑和连续7次率领了海上远征探险的壮举,访问了40多个国家。

　　郑和的船队由三百艘大船及三万多名水兵组成。船队中最大的一艘船被称为"宝船",其船身长达133米,船桅多达九根,可搭载一千人。郑和率领汉族与穆斯林船员一起打开了中国在非洲、印度及东南亚的贸易航线。

　　这几次远航刺激了外国对中国货物如丝绸、瓷器等的兴趣。此外,郑和也将外国的珍奇宝物带回中国,包括以前没见过的麒麟(长颈鹿)。同时,郑和船队显而易见的强大阵容,使中国皇帝获得了亚洲各国的敬畏。

　　郑和下西洋的主要目的在于宣扬大明的强盛国威,但他经常卷入出访地的政治。例如,在锡兰(即今天的斯里兰卡),他扶持合法统治者重登王位。在苏门答腊岛(今天印尼的一部分),郑和击退一支由残暴海盗领军的队伍,并将其首领押回中国处死。

　　郑和于公元1433年去世,可能葬身于汪洋大海之中,但江苏省现在仍有他的坟墓和一座小型纪念碑。郑和死后3年,新登基的皇帝下诏禁止远洋船舶的建造,中国这短暂的海军扩张时代也就到此结束了。中国的政策转而向内,把大海完全拱手让给欧洲新兴的国家。

　　中国的政策为何会发生这样的转变,一直众说纷纭。不管是什么原因,朝中保守势力占了上风,这样中国统治世界的潜力终究未能得到发挥。郑和令人惊叹的航海纪录也遭焚毁湮灭。直到20世纪初叶,中国才有另一支相当规模的船队驶向大海。

 **Notes**

本文选自网络有声阅读库"A treasure ship captain." http://www.wwenglish.com/en/club/read/11974.htm. 作者匿名。

Word Bank

船队	fleet	起航	set sail
航行	voyages	探险家	adventurer
水手辛巴达	Sinbad the Sailor	净身	castrate
太监	eunuch	贸易航线	trade routes
宝船	treasure ships	强盛国威	superiority
保守势力	conservative forces	纪念碑	monument

Directions: Please summarize the passage in English. Your summary should be about 150—200 words.

Passage B

The First Voyage—Discovery of the New Land

Edward Everett Hale

At last all was ready. That is to say, the fleet was so far ready that Columbus was ready to start. The vessels were small, as we think of vessels, but he was not dissatisfied. He says in the beginning of his journal, "I armed three vessels very fit for such an enterprise." He had left Grenada as late as the twelfth of May. He had crossed Spain to Palos, and in less than three months had fitted out the ships and was ready for sea.

The harbor of Palos is now ruined. Mud and gravel, brought down by the River Tinto, have filled up the bay, so that even small boats cannot approach the shore. The traveler finds, however, the island of Saltes, quite outside the bay, much as Columbus left it. It is a small spit of sand, covered with shells and with a few seashore herbs. His own account of the great voyage begins with the words: "Friday, August 3, 1492. Set sail from the bar of Saltes at 8 o'clock, and proceeded with a strong breeze till sunset sixty miles, or fifteen leagues south, afterward southwest and south by west, which is in the direction of the Canaries." It appears, therefore, that the great voyage, the most important and successful ever made, began on Friday, the day which is said to be so much disliked by sailors. Columbus never alludes to this superstition.

He had always meant to sail first for the Canaries, which were the most western land then known in the latitude of his voyage. From Lisbon to the famous city of "Quisay" or "Quinsay" in Asia, Toscanelli, his learned correspondent, supposed the distance to be less than one thousand leagues westward. From the Canary islands, on that supposition, the distance would be ten degrees less. The distance to Cipango, or Japan, would be much less.

...

With the eleventh of October, came certainty. The eleventh is sometimes spoken of as the day of discovery, and sometimes the twelfth, when they landed on the first island of the new world.

The whole original record of the discovery is this: "Oct. 11, course to west and southwest. Heavier sea than they had known, pardelas and a green branch near the caravel of the Admiral." From the Pinta they see a branch of a tree, a stake and a smaller stake, which they draw in, and which appears to have been cut with iron, and a piece of cane. Besides these, there is a land shrub and a little bit of board. The crew of the Nina saw other signs of land and a branch covered with thorns and flowers. With these tokens every-one breathes again and is delighted. They sail twenty-seven leagues on this course.

The Admiral orders that they shall resume a westerly course at sunset. They make twelve miles each hour; up till two hours after midnight they made ninety miles.

"The Pinta, the best sailer of the three, was ahead. She makes signals, already agreed upon, that she has discovered land." A sailor named Rodrigo de Triana was the first to see this land. For the Admiral being on the castle of the poop of the ship at ten at night really saw a light, but it was so shut in by darkness that he did not like to say that it was a sign of land. Still he called up Pedro Gutierrez, the king's chamberlain, and said to him that there seemed to be a light, and asked him to look. He did so and saw it. He said the same to Rodrigo Sanchez of Segovia, who had been sent by the king and queen as inspector in the fleet, but he saw nothing, being indeed in a place where he could see nothing.

Unit 2

"After the Admiral spoke of it, the light was seen once or twice. It was like a wax candle, raised and lowered, which would appear to few to be a sign of land. But the Admiral was certain that it was a sign of land." Therefore when they said the "Salve," which all the sailors are used to say and sing in their fashion, the Admiral ordered them to look out well from the forecastle, and he would give at once a silk jacket to the man who first saw land, besides the other rewards which the sovereigns had ordered, which were 10,000 maravedis, to be paid as an annuity forever to the man who saw it first.

"At two hours after midnight land appeared, from which they were about two leagues off."

This is the one account of the discovery written at the time. It is worth copying and reading at full in its little details, for it contrasts curiously with the embellished accounts which appear in the next generation. Thus the historian Oviedo says, in a dramatic way:

"One of the ship boys on the largest ship, a native of Lepe, cried 'Fire!' 'Land!' Immediately a servant of Columbus replied, 'The Admiral had said that already.' Soon after, Columbus said, 'I said so some time ago, and that I saw that fire on the land.'" And so indeed it happened that Thursday, at two hours after midnight, the Admiral called a gentleman named Escobedos, officer of the wardrobe of the king, and told him that he saw fire. And at the break of day, at the time Columbus had predicted the day before, they saw from the largest ship the island which the Indians call Guanahani to the north of them.

"And the first man to see the land, when day came, was Rodrigo of Triana, on the eleventh day of October, 1492." Nothing is more certain than that this was really on the twelfth.

The reward for first seeing land was eventually awarded to Columbus, and it was regularly paid him through his life. It was the annual payment of 10,000 maravedis. A maravedi was then a little less than six cents of our currency. The annuity was, therefore, about six hundred dollars a year. The worth of a maravedi varied, from time to time, so that the calculations of the value of any number of maravedis are very confusing. Before the coin went out of use it was worth only half a cent.

Notes

1. This passage was selected from the book entitled *The Life of Christopher Columbus from His Own Letters and Journals* by Edward Everett Hale, published in 1892.
2. Edward Everett Hale (April 3, 1822—June 10, 1909) was an American author, historian and Unitarian minister. He published a wide variety of works in fiction, history and biography. He used his writings and the two magazines he founded, *Old and New* (1870—1875) and *Lend a Hand* (1886—1897), to advance a number of social reforms, including religious tolerance, the abolition of slavery and wider education.

Directions: Please summarize the passage in Chinese. Your summary should be about 200—300 words.

Unit 3

PHILOSOPHY AND LIFE

The art of living is to know when to hold fast and when to let go. For life is a paradox: it enjoins us to cling to its many gifts even while it ordains their eventual relinquishment.

Don't spend and waste your lives accumulating objects that will only turn to dust and ashes. Pursue not so much the material as the ideal, for ideals alone invest life with meaning and are of enduring worth.

—*From Two Truths to Live By*

Learning Objectives

Upon the completion of this unit, you should be able to

Remembering & Understanding	★ read Text A and Text B aloud smoothly with expression indicative of comprehension and tone; ★ identify and explain in your own words the thesis and the major points of Text A and Ttext B;
Analyzing & Applying	★ learn to use affixes to enlarge your vocabulary; ★ make reference to the thesis and/or the major points of Text A and Text B in your writing; ★ grasp some useful sentence structures in your writing;
Evaluating & Creating	★ support your thesis statement by example(s) in expository writing; ★ reflect on the thesis and major points of Text B and develop your critical thinking; ★ deliver a clear and coherent oral presentation of your views on success and happiness in life.

Unit 3

Part One Lead-in

Section 1 Listening: True Success

Task 1 Filling the Blanks

Directions: Please fill in the blanks with one or two words on the basis of what you have heard.

True success is not about _____ acquisition. It's about what I like to call The 3-D Approach to Life:

Discover your positive talents.

Develop the most meaningful and beneficial of those talents.

Deploy your talents into the world for the good of others as well as yourself.

I say that it is important to discover your positive talents. By "positive," I mean talents that can make a positive, meaningful, beneficial _____ to your life, or to the lives of others. I mean talents whose exercise will _____ the best about life and cohere with all that we know to be good and important. I _____ also that you should develop the most meaningful and beneficial of those talents. Life is short. Time is _____. Energy is limited. We should all focus on the highest of our talents, if we want true success in our lives.

The great German philosopher Leibniz (1646—1716) tells a story about a man who cultivates expertise at throwing peas and skewering(刺穿)them on pins. A person might have a talent for doing this, but it doesn't follow _____ that he should spend a lot of time cultivating that skill. It is a waste of time. You might have a talent for insulting people, but it's not one you should cultivate, or even discover. Insulting people is not a positive, meaningful, beneficial talent. We should discover and cultivate what is best within ourselves. And we should spend _____ time on only those talents that can be put to work somehow for the good of others as well as ourselves.

True success is deeply satisfying success. True success is _____ success. It is a form of achievement that nurtures the whole person. It is not _____ or essentially detrimental(有害的) to others. It will have different forms for different people. But it will always _____ the 3-D approach at its core.

Task 2 Group Discussion

Directions: Please discuss the following questions in pairs or groups based on what you have heard.

1. What positive talents do you discover in yourself?
2. How do you put your positive talents to work for the good of other people and yourself?
3. What is your understanding of true success?

Section 2 Watching: Less Stuff, More Happiness

Task 1 Group Discussion

Directions: Please watch the video clip "Less Stuff, More Happiness" and discuss the following questions in pairs or groups.

1. What do less stuff and less space equal, according to the speaker?
2. What approaches does the speaker advise to us in order to make us live little?
3. What is your understanding of "Less Stuff, More Happiness"?

Task 2 Retelling

Directions: Please watch the video clip again, and try to retell how the speaker makes the spaces and housewares in his apartment multifunctional.

Part Two   Reading and Writing

Text A

Two Truths to Live By

Hold Fast and Let go: Understand this paradox,
and you stand at the very gate of wisdom.

Alexander M. Schindler

1 The art of living is to know when to hold fast and when to let go. For life is a **paradox**: it enjoins us to **cling to** its many gifts even while it ordains their eventual relinquishment（放弃）.The rabbis of old put it this way: "A man comes to this world with his fist **clenched**, but when he dies, his hand is open."

2 Surely we ought to hold fast to life, for it is **wondrous**, and full of a beauty that breaks through every **pore** of God's own earth. We know that this is so, but all too often we recognize this truth only in our backward glance when we remember what it was and then suddenly realize that it is no more.

3 We remember a beauty that faded, a love that **waned**. But we remember with far great pain that we did not see that beauty when it flowered, that we failed to respond with love when it was **tendered**.

4 A recent experience re-taught me this truth. I was **hospitalized** following a severe heart attack and had been in intensive care for days. It was not a pleasant place.

5 One morning, I had to have some additional tests. The required machines were located in a building at the opposite end of the hospital, so I had to be wheeled across the courtyard on a gurney（轮床）.

6 As we emerged from our unit, the sunlight hit me. That's all there was to my

experience. Just the light of the sun. And yet how beautiful it was—how warming, how sparkling, how brilliant!

7   I looked to see whether anyone else *relished* the sun's golden glow, but everyone was hurrying *to and fro*, most with eyes fixed on the ground. Then I remembered how often I, too, had been indifferent to the *grandeur* of each day, too *preoccupied* with *petty* and sometimes even mean concerns to *respond to* the *splendor* of it all.

8   The insight *gleaned* from that experience is really as commonplace as was the experience itself: life's gifts are precious—but we are too *heedless* of them.

9   Here then is the first pole of life's *paradoxical* demands on us: Never too busy for the wonder and the awe of life. Be reverent before each dawning day. Embrace each hour. Seize each golden minute.

10 Hold fast to life, but not so fast that you cannot let go. This is the second side of life's coin, the opposite pole of its paradox: we must accept our losses, and learn how to let go.

11 This is not an easy lesson to learn, especially when we are young and think that the world is ours to command, that whatever we desire with the full force of our *passionate* being can, nay, will, be ours. But then life moves along to confront us with realities, and slowly but surely this second truth *dawns upon* us.

12 At every stage of life we sustain losses—and grow in the process. We begin our independent lives only when we emerge from the *womb* and lose its protective shelter. We enter a progression of schools; then we leave our mothers and fathers and our childhood homes. We get married and have children and then have to let them go. We confront the death of our parents and our spouses. We face the gradual or not so gradual waning of our own strength. And ultimately, as the parable of the open and closed hand suggests, we must confront the *inevitability* of our own demise (死亡), losing ourselves, as it were, all that we were or dreamed to be.

13 But why should we *be reconciled to* life's *contradictory* demands? Why fashion things of beauty when beauty is evanescent (逐渐消失的)? Why give our heart in love when those we love will ultimately be torn from our grasp?

14 In order to resolve this paradox, we must seek a wider perspective, viewing our lives as through windows that open on eternity. Once we do that, we realize that though our lives are finite, our deeds on earth weave a timeless pattern.

15 Life is never just being. It's a becoming, a *relentless* flowing on. Our parents live on through us, and we will live on through our children. The institutions we build endure, and we will endure through them. The beauty we fashion cannot be dimmed by death. Our flesh may *perish*; our hands will *wither*, but that which they create in beauty and goodness and truth lives on for all time to come.

16 Don't spend and waste your lives *accumulating* objects that will only turn to dust and ashes. Pursue not so much the material as the ideal, for ideals alone invest life with meaning and are of enduring worth.

17 Add love to a house and you have a home. Add *righteousness* to a city and you have

a community. Add truth to a pile of red brick and you have school. Add religion to the humblest of edifices(建筑物)and you have a *sanctuary*. Add justice to the *far-flung* round of human *endeavor* and you have civilization. Put them all together, exalt them above their present imperfections, add to them the vision of human kind *redeemed,* forever free of need and *strife* and you have a future lighted with the colors of hope.

New Words

paradox	[ˈpærədɒks]	n.	(logic) a statement that contradicts itself 悖论,反论
clench	[klentʃ]	v.	hold sth. tightly and firmly 捏紧,攥紧,握紧
wondrous	[ˈwʌndrəs]	a.	(literary) good or impressive in a surprising way （文）奇妙的,令人惊叹的
pore	[pɔr]	n.	the very small holes in your skin that sweat can pass through; one of the similar small holes in the surface of a plant or a rock (皮肤上的)毛孔,孔隙
wane	[wen]	v.	become weaker and lesser (in size or strength or power or number) 衰落,变小,亏缺
tender	[ˈtɛndɚ]	v.	offer or present for acceptance; propose a payment 提供,偿还
hospitalize	[ˈhɒspitəlaiz]	v.	admit into a hospital 就医,送……进医院治疗
relish	[ˈrɛlɪʃ]	v.	derive or receive pleasure from; get enjoyment from; take pleasure in 期待,享受,品味
grandeur	[ˈgrændʒɚ]	n.	the quality of being magnificent or splendid or grand 壮丽,庄严,宏伟
preoccupy	[priːˈɒkjupai]	v.	engage or engross the interest or attention of beforehand or occupy urgently or obsessively 迷住,使全神贯注
petty	[ˈpeti]	a.	small and of little importance 琐碎的,小气的
splendor	[ˈsplɛndɚ]	n.	the quality of being magnificent or splendid or grand 光彩,壮丽
glean	[glin]	v.	gather, collect 收集(资料),拾(落穗)
heedless	[ˈhiːdlis]	a.	marked by or paying little heed or attention 不注意的,不留心的
paradoxical	[ˌpærəˈdɒksikəl]	a.	seemingly contradictory but nonetheless possibly true 矛盾的,诡论的,似非而是的
passionate	[ˈpæʃənit]	a.	having or expressing strong emotions 热情的,热烈的,激昂的
womb	[wum]	n.	a hollow muscular organ in the pelvic cavity of females 子宫

Unit 3

inevitability	[inˌevitəˈbiləti]	n.	the quality of being unavoidable 必然性,不可逃避
reconcile	[ˈrekənsail]	v.	make compatible with 使和解,调解,使顺从
contradictory	[ˌkɔntrəˈdiktəri]	a.	containing or showing a contradiction 相互矛盾的，对立的,不一致的
relentless	[riˈlentlis]	a.	never-ceasing 无情的,残酷的,不间断的
perish	[ˈperiʃ]	v.	pass from physical life and lose all bodily attributes and functions necessary to sustain life 死亡,毁灭
wither	[ˈwiðə]	v.	lose freshness, vigor, or vitality 枯萎,凋谢
accumulate	[əˈkjuːmjuleit]	v.	get or gather together 累积,积聚
righteousness	[ˈraitʃəsnis]	n.	morally right and good 正义,正直
sanctuary	[ˈsæŋktjuˈri]	n.	a consecrated place where sacred objects are kept; a shelter from danger or hardship 避难所,神殿
far-flung	[ˈfɑːˈflʌŋ]	a.	spread over a wide area 广泛的,分布广的
endeavor	[inˈdevə]	n.	a purposeful or industrious undertaking (esp. one that requires effort or boldness) 努力,尽力
redeem	[riˈdiːm]	v.	save from sins; restore the honor or worth of 赎回,救赎
strife	[straif]	n.	strong disagreement or fighting; lack of agreement or harmony 冲突,争吵,不和

Phrases & Expressions

cling to	hold tightly to 紧握不放
to and fro	backwards and forwards 来回地
respond to	react quickly or in the correct way to sth. 反应灵敏,作出正确反应
dawn on/upon	realize sth. for the first time 使……开始明白,顿悟
reconcile sb./oneself to sth.	make sb./oneself accept a difficult or unpleasant situation 使接受[困难或不愉快的情况],顺从,妥协

Notes

1. The text was adapted from a commencement speech at the University of South Carolina in 1987 by Alexander M. Schindler.
2. Alexander M. Schindler(1925—2000), born in Munich, Germany, was a rabbi and the leading figure of American Jewry and Reform Judaism during the 1970s and 1980s. He served as president of the Union of American Hebrew Congregations (since renamed the Union for Reform Judaism) from 1973 to 1996. He served as chairman of the Conference of Presidents of Major American Jewish Organizations.

Task 1　Generating the Outline

Directions: Please identify the thesis of the passage and the main point of each paragraph, and then find out how these points develop the thesis. You may use the table below for your help.

Para. 1: The thesis	The art of living lies in two truths:_____.
Paras. 2—3: The first truth	Surely we ought to hold fast to life, but all too often we recognize this truth _____.
Paras. 4—7: An example	A recent experience re-taught me this truth. I was _____, I had to have _____, so I had to be wheeled across the courtyard. The sunlight hit me, and I looked to see whether anyone else relished the sun's golden glow, but _____.
Paras. 8—9: Conclusion	Life's gifts are precious—but _____. The first pole of life's paradoxical demands on us is _____.
Para. 10: The second truth	The opposite pole of life's paradox is _____.
Paras. 11—12: Illustration	To let go is not an easy lesson to learn. But slowly and surely this truth _____. At every stage we sustain losses—and_____.
Paras. 13—15: Analysis	To resolve the paradox of life, we must seek_____.
Paras. 16—17: Advice	Pursue not so much the material as the ideal, for _____.

Task 2　Understanding the Text

Directions: Please answer the following questions based on Text A.

1. Why does the author say that life is a paradox?
2. What does "hold fast to life" mean according to the author? Give your understanding with an example.
3. When do people begin to realize the truth that they should hold fast to life?
4. Why did the author appreciate the beauty of the sun's golden glow so much one day?
5. Why do you think people are so indifferent to the grandeur of each day?
6. What did the author learn from his recent experience?
7. What does "let go" mean according to the author? Give your understanding with an example.
8. How do people accept losses and learn how to let go at every stage of life?
9. What does the author mean by saying "Life is never just being. It's a becoming, a relentless flowing on"?
10. What kind of life do you think is more meaningful and worth living?

Task 3　Vocabulary Building

Directions: The suffix -ize can be added to nouns or adjectives to form verbs that describe the process by which a state, quality, or condition is brought about.

$$\text{hospital+ize} \to \text{hospitalize} \quad \text{normal + ize} \to \text{normalize}$$

Study the words ending with -ize given below and complete the following sentences with them. Change the form where necessary.

> symbolize   industrialize   apologize   revolutionize   philosophize   recognize

1. Most of us fail to _____ the debt we owe to these shoots of difficulty. We are liable to think that anxiety and envy have nothing legitimate to teach us and so remove them like emotional weeds.
2. Statistics from ten _____ countries found that women employed in regular jobs worked about 20 percent longer hours than regularly employed men.
3. In the painting he was finishing a philosophical point while at the same time reaching serenely for the hemlock that would end his life, _____ both his obedience to the laws of Athens and allegiance to his calling.
4. In calmer moments, the angry may _____ and explain that they were overwhelmed by a power stronger than themselves, that is, stronger than their reason.
5. Socrates did his _____ orally, in the company of other people—and not always in the company of people who were enjoying the journey with him.
6. New technology is going to _____ everything we do.

Directions: The suffix -less can be added to nouns or verbs to form adjectives with the meaning "without" "not doing; not affected by".

> heed +less → heedless, relent +less → relentless, time +less → timeless

> homeless   sleepless   countless   senseless   colorless   ceaseless

1. In his speeches the mayor always puts on a big show of crocodile tears for poor and _____ people. But I don't see him doing anything to help them.
2. I've had a few _____ nights recently, lying awake and thinking how to free myself from expectations which inspire bitterness.
3. A two-hour drive north of Beijing's oppressive smog and _____ high-rises, the town provides a surreal sense of escape.
4. The new treatment could save Emma's life and the lives of _____ others.
5. The _____ anti-corruption campaign shows the government's determination to fight against corruption.
6. Schopenhauer read of ants, beetles, bees, flies, grasshoppers, moles and migratory birds, and observed, with compassion and puzzlement, how all these creatures displayed an ardent, _____ commitment to life.

Task 4 Learning the Phrases

Directions: Please fill in the blanks in the sentences below with the phrases listed in the box. Change the forms if necessary. Notice that some phrases need to be used more than once.

> cling to   be indifferent to   respond to
> dawn on   reconcile sb. to sth.   be preoccupied with

1. The old mother _____ the belief that her son was still alive though she was told that the missing flight had ended in the Ocean.
2. For a long time it had seemed to me that life was about to begin—real life. But there was always some obstacle in the way, something to be gotten through first, some unfinished business, time still to be served, a debt to be paid. Then life would begin. At last it _____ me that these obstacles were my life.
3. After they had a quarrel, Susan didn't _____ any of his boyfriend's email.
4. It slowly _____ him that he should learn when enough is enough and when it isn't.
5. She is completely _____ all the wedding preparations at the moment, and has no time to run her store.
6. Freud argued that philosophy _____ the tradition methods of creating illusion about the universe without giving much thought to the intuitions which determine the most coherent picture of the universe.
7. The government cannot afford to _____ public opinion.
8. Philosophy must _____ us _____ the true dimensions of reality, and so spare us, if not frustration itself, then at least its panoply of harmful accompanying emotions.
9. _____ the news that a black young man was shot by a policeman, Mr. Watt appealed for calm.
10. Why should a woman _____ being a housewife, taking care of her children and husband all year round at home?

Task 5 Studying the Sentence Structure

Sentences with "imperative+and+ a clause" structure

Sentences from the text

1. Understand this paradox, and you stand at the very gate of wisdom. (Subtitle)
2. Add love to a house and you have a home. Add righteousness to a city and you have a community. Add truth to a pile of red brick and you have school. Add religion to the humblest of edifices and you have a sanctuary. Add justice to the far-flung round of human endeavor and you have civilization. (Para. 17)

Directions: Please follow the examples and rewrite the following sentences, using the "imperative + and + a clause" structure.

Tips

1. The "imperative+and+ a clause" structure can be used to replace *if* clause to warn or advise sb. that sth. could happen.
2. A comma can be used before the conjunction.

1. If you work late tonight, I will pay you well.

_____

2. If you arrive late once more, you'll be fired.

_____

Unit 3

3. It you work hard, you'll pass the examinations.

4. If you turn on TV, you will see the breaking news on almost all channels.

Task 6 Paraphrasing Difficult Sentences

1. We know that this is so, but all too often we recognize this truth only in our backward glance when we remember what it was and then suddenly realize that it is no more.

2. But then life moves along to confront us with realities, and slowly but surely this second truth dawns upon us.

3. Life is never just being. It's a becoming, a relentless flowing on.

4. Pursue not so much the material as the ideal, for ideals alone invest life with meaning and are of enduring worth.

5. Put them all together, exalt them above their present imperfections, add to them the vision of human kind redeemed, forever free of need and strife and you have a future lighted with the colors of hope.

Task 7 Summarizing the Text

Directions: Please summarize Text A in 150 words. You may use the table in Task 1 to help you.

Task 8 Writing with Example(s)

Directions: Write an essay of about 200 words in 3 paragraphs on My View on Facing Setbacks in University. In the first paragraph, you should begin with the thesis statement, then you should support your view with some examples. Each body paragraph may develop a separate example. You may use what is provided in the box below to help you.

Tips

1. Examples and illustrations are often used in explaining an idea or an opinion we hold, the use of detailed examples can make abstract ideas concrete and general opinion more specific. Well-chosen examples can make our writing vivid and convincing.

2. Examples and illustrations are drawn from our experience, our observation, and our reading. For instance, in Text A the author states his first view that surely we ought to hold fast to life in paragraph 2, then he supports his view by giving an example of his own experience and

observation from paragraph 4 to 8.

1. What is your view on facing setbacks in university?
2. What setbacks have you had since you came to university?
3. How did you overcome them?

Part Three   Reading and Speaking

Text B

What is Enough? The Race for More
Tom Morris

1   We live in an *acquisitive* culture. We have more, and we want more, than ever before. We live in a time of *boundless* opportunity. But we also live in an age filled with lives out of control. We spend all our time and energy chasing things that won't satisfy us. Why?

2   The greatest case of mistaken *identity* in the modern world has involved the four *markers* of public success: money, fame, power and status. These four things just may have been the most widely shared dreams and the most *ardently* pursued goals in the past century. Yet, as an ancient *philosopher* might say, they can make very good servants, but are themselves very bad masters.

3   Money, fame, power and status can be good and useful as resources, but they are very problematic as focal goals. When they are pursued as focal targets, the concept of "enough" can't get a *grip* at all. What amount of money is enough? Everyone I know who has a little wants more. But it's even more interesting that everyone I know who has a lot wants even more. A reporter once asked John D. Rockefeller how much money it takes for a man to be happy. He replied, "A little bit more than he's got."

4   What is enough? The concept of enough is, of course, a relative concept. Any question of what would be enough begs the follow-up question "Enough for what?" And this just shows that the concept of enough applies only to things that are of *instrumental* value, valuable only *insofar* as they lead to or produce something else (something that itself either also has instrumental value, or else has *intrinsic* value, value in and of itself).

5   Put simply, the question of enough applies only to things that are *in some sense* resources. When money, fame, power, and status are viewed as resources, the question of enough does have application. Enough money is the amount of money it takes to complete a project, or *pay off* debts. Or maintain a lifestyle. Enough power is

the amount it takes to get a job done. Even fame and status can work this way. For an actor, enough fame is the amount that gets him invited to work in good movies for healthy fees and then gets public attention for his work. A certain level of status in a community can be judged enough for playing a particular role in a community affairs or for producing a certain degree of *receptivity* in people concerning a project or process that needs support.

6   Enough is a relative concept. More is absolute. There can always be more. And that's a problem for many people. We live in a very *competitive* culture, so we live in a culture of more. It's nearly heretical(异端的)to suggest that bigger is not always better and faster is not always an improvement. I don't need a Ferrari to get me home from the grocery store. Ice cream doesn't melt that fast. How big should a company be? How powerful a computer do I need? How many items of clothing are enough? Or, *closer to home* for me, how many guitars do I actually need to own? Are there lines to be *drawn*? In a culture of more, it's often hard to see or set limits.

7   There are two different forms of dissatisfaction in human life. There is first the dissatisfaction of *acquisition*. This is when you're not satisfied with what you have. You want more stuff. More money. More power. A bigger house. Another house. A more luxurious car. Or a faster car.

8   The second form of dissatisfaction is the dissatisfaction of *aspiration*. This is when you are not satisfied with what you are and want to become something better. You want to be wiser, to know more, to experience more, to develop more talents, to be a better person. You want to deepen yourself spiritually. You want to connect better with your world. You want to have a deeper impact for good on your children, on your community, or in your work. You *aspire to* a richer, more fulfilling being-in-the-world.

9   The dissatisfaction of acquisition *feeds on* itself in an almost cancerous way. The more you *give in to* it and try to satisfy it, the more it can grow, until it is literally out of control. There are people who can fully enjoy owning the new Mercedes *convertible* that they long *lusted* for only to the moment when that new red Ferrari *pulls up* beside them at a stoplight. The dissatisfaction of acquisition can become an unhealthy, impossible, *tyrannical* demand.

10 The dissatisfaction of aspiration can be quite different. Contentment is not supposed to be the same things as apathy(淡漠). Contentment is emotionally accepting your present as being what it is, without being filled with *resentment*, frustration, or *irritation* at anything you are undergoing. But that is thoroughly *compatible* with wanting the future to be quite different. You aspire to be better or to accomplish more. You are not satisfied to stay where you are existentially with no further growth and no further effects for good on your world. You want to be and do more. This is the dissatisfaction of aspiration. It can be a very healthy goad(激励)to personal growth and fulfillment.

11 Is there a certain number of books, such that, having read that many, you will have read enough? Is there a total number of ideas such that, having had that many

new thoughts, you will be able to say, "Enough, already"? Isn't personal growth and aspiration at least *in principle* open-ended in a way that acquisition is not? I have enough tennis shoes. I have enough suits. I have enough computers. But in the *confines* of this life, I'll never be wise enough. And that's no *tragedy* at all. I'm a joyful guy, but I'll never have my fill of joy—I'll never be joyful enough. But don't feel sorry for me about that.

12   In fact, it is the materially *well off* among us who feel wise enough already, but want much more stuff, who are living the *philosophical* tragedy of our times. To those men and women I want to say: Learn when enough is enough and when it isn't. The external things that we accrue(获得) can be great resources for the inner journey we are on, as well as for making our outer mark on the world, if we have enough guidance along the way to know what it's worth our time and energy to pursue.

New Words

acquisitive	[əˈkwɪzɪtɪv]	a.	eager to acquire and possess things especially material possessions or ideas 贪得的,想获得的,可学到的
boundless	[ˈbaundlis]	a.	without limits; seeming to have no end 无限的;无止境的
identity	[aiˈdentəti]	n.	who or what sb./sth. is 身份,本身,本体
marker	[ˈmɑːkər]	n.	some conspicuous object used to distinguish or mark sth.; a distinguishing symbol 书签,标识物
ardently	[ˈɑːdəntli]	ad.	enthusiastically eagerly 热烈地,热心地
philosopher	[fiˈlɔsəfə]	n.	a specialist in philosophy 哲学家,哲人
grip	[grip]	n.	an understanding of sth. 理解,了解
instrumental	[ˌinstruˈmentəl]	a.	important in making sth. happen 起重要作用的
insofar	[ˌinsəuˈfɑː]	ad.	to the degree or extent that 在……的范围,到这种程度
intrinsic	[inˈtrinsik]	a.	belonging to a thing by its very nature 本质的,固有的
receptivity	[risepˈtiviti]	n.	willingness or readiness to receive (especially impressions or ideas) 接受能力,感受性
competitive	[kəmˈpetitiv]	a.	involving competition or competitiveness 竞争的,求胜心切的
acquisition	[ˌækwiˈziʃən]	n.	the act of contracting or assuming or acquiring possession of sth. 获得

Unit 3

aspiration	[ˌæspəˈreɪʃ(ə)n]	n.	a will to succeed a cherished desire 渴望，抱负，志向
convertible	[kənˈvɜːtəbl]	n.	a car that has top that can be folded or removed 有活动折篷的汽车，敞篷汽车
lust	[lʌst]	v.	have a craving, appetite, or great desire for 贪求，渴望
tyrannical	[tɪˈrænɪkəl]	a.	of or relating to or associated with or resembling a dictatorship; marked by unjust severity or arbitrary behavior; characteristic of an absolute ruler or absolute rule; having absolute sovereignty 专横的，残暴的
resentment	[rɪˈzentmənt]	n.	a feeling of deep and bitter anger and ill-will 愤恨，怨恨
irritation	[ˌɪrɪˈteɪʃn]	n.	the psychological state of being irritated or annoyed; a sudden outburst of anger 激怒，恼怒；令人恼火的事
compatible	[kəmˈpætəbl]	a.	able to exist and perform in harmonious or agreeable combination 兼容的，能共处的，可并立的
confines	[ˈkɒnfaɪnz]	n.	limits or borders 范围，界限，边界
tragedy	[ˈtrædʒɪdɪ]	n.	an event resulting in great loss and misfortune 悲剧，灾难，惨案
philosophical	[ˌfɪləˈsɒfɪkəl]	a.	connected with philosophy 哲学的

Phrases & Expressions

in some sense	in one way or some ways 在某种意义上 在某种程度上
pay sth. off	finish paying money owed for sth. 还清，付清
close to home	if sth. unpleasant happens close to home, you are directly affected by it (令人不愉快的事)发生在自己身边的，直接影响到自身的
draw the line	allow or accept sth. up to a particular point, but not beyond it 给(某事)划定出界限
aspire to	(sth./to do sth.) desire and work towards achieving sth. important 渴望(成就)；有志(成为)
feed on	(often disapproving) become stronger because of sth. else 因……而壮大；从……中得到滋养
give in to	no longer to try to stop yourself from doing sth. you want to do 克制；屈服于

pull up	(of a vehicle or its driver) stop （车辆或司机）停车
in principle	if sth. is possible in principle, there is no good reason why it should not happen, but it has not actually happened yet 原则上，在理论上，按道理
well off	having a lot of money 富裕的，富有的

 Notes

1. This article is adapted from the book *Philosophy for Dummies* published by Wiley Publishing, Inc. in 1999.

2. The author, Tom Morris, is the author of *If Aristotle Ran General Motors: The New Soul of Business* published in 1997. He holds a Ph.D. in both Philosophy and Religious Studies from Yale University and for 15 years served as a Professor of Philosophy at the University of Notre Dame. This scholar is a former rock guitarist. He is now Chairman of the Morris Institute for Human Values in Wilmington, North Carolina.

3. John D. Rockefeller: John Davison Rockefeller, Sr. (July 8, 1839—May 23, 1937) an American business magnate and philanthropist. He was a co-founder of the Standard Oil Company, which dominated the oil industry. In 1870, he founded Standard Oil Company, which became Standard Oil Trust in 1892. Rockefeller actively ran it until he officially retired in 1897. The Trust was broken up by the Supreme Court in 1911.

Task 1 Summarizing

Directions: Fill in the blanks in the following text outline with key points based on an overall understanding and then make an oral summary.

1. We live in an acquisitive culture. But we also lie in an age filled with lives out of control.
2. The greatest case of mistaken identity in the modern world _____.
3. Enough is a relative concept, which applies only to _____.
4. More is an absolute concept, because _____.
5. There are two forms of dissatisfaction:
   a. _____
   b. _____
6. Advice given to those who want more stuff: _____.

Task 2 Reflecting on the Text

Directions: Discuss the following questions with your partner and then give an oral presentation of your reflections on the text. You may organize your presentation by linking up your answers to the questions.

Guiding Questions:

1. Are you satisfied with what you have?
2. Will you spend all your time and energy pursuing money, fame, power and status? Why or why not?
3. What is your understanding of the concept of enough?
4. What do you think are the differences between the two forms of dissatisfaction in human life?

5. Have you learned when enough is enough and when it isn't after reading the text?

Task 3   Making a Presentation

Directions: Give an oral presentation of your views on the following topics centering around " Success and Happiness in Life." You should state your view clearly in the beginning, and then support your view with evidence.

1. Self-knowledge is the prerequisite for any rational road to success and happiness.
2. What is the good life?

Below are some words and expressions that you might find useful in your presentation.

1) require	2) reflect on
3) examine	4) satisfy
5) Only by doing sth. can one...	6) involve
7) obstacle	8) external things
9) spiritual needs	10) achieve

Part Four   Cross Cultural Communication

Passage A

人生的爱好者：陶渊明

林语堂

  我们晓得如果我们把积极的和消极的人生观念适当地混合起来，我们能够得到一种和谐的中庸哲学，介于动作与不动作之间；介于尘世徒然的匆忙与完全逃避人生责任之间；在世界上的一切哲学之中，这一种可说是人类生活上最健全最美满的理想了。还有一点更加重要，就是这两种不同的观念的混合，产生了一种和谐的人格；这种和谐的人格便是一切文化和教育的公认目的。我们在这种和谐的人格中，看见一种人生的欢快和爱好，这是值得注意的。

  要我描写这种人生的爱好的性质是很困难的；用一个比喻来说明，或叙述一位人生的爱好者的真实事迹，是比较容易的。陶渊明，这位中国最伟大的诗人和中国文化上最和谐的产物，很自然地浮上我的心头。当我说陶渊明是中国整个文学传统上最和谐最完美的人物时，一定没有一个中国人会反对我的话的。他不曾做过大官，没有权利和外表的成就，除一部薄薄的诗集和三四篇散文之外，也不曾留给我们什么文学遗产，可是他至今日依然是一堆照澈古今的烽火，在那些较渺小的诗人和作家心目中，他永远是最高人格的象征。他的生活是简朴的，风格也是简朴的，这种简朴的特质是令人敬畏的，是会使那些较聪明较熟悉世故的人自惭形秽的。他今日是人生的真爱好者的模范，因为他心中反抗尘世欲望的念头，并没有驱使他去做一个彻底的遁世者，反而使他和感官的生活调和起来。文学的浪漫主义，与道家的闲散生活和反抗儒家的教义，已经在中国活动了两百多年，而和前世纪的儒家哲学合并起来，造就这么一种和谐的人格。在陶渊明的身上，我们看到那种积极的人生观已经丧失其愚蠢的满足，而那种玩世的哲学也已经丧失其尖刻的叛逆性(我们在托洛/梭罗的身上还可以看到这么一种特质——这是一个不朽的标志)，而人类的智慧第一次在宽容的嘲弄的精神中达到成熟期了。

在我的心目中，陶渊明代表中国文化的一种奇特的特质，这种特质就是肉的专一和灵的傲慢的奇怪混合，就是不流于灵欲的精神生活和不流于肉欲的物质生活的奇怪混合；在这种混合中，感官和心灵是和谐相处的。因为理想的哲学家能够了解女人的妩媚而不流于粗鄙，能够酷爱人生而不过度，能够看见尘世的成功和失败的空虚，能够站在超越人生和脱离人生的地位，而不敌视人生。因为陶渊明已经达到了那种心灵发展的真正和谐的境地，所以我们看不见一丝一毫的内心冲突，所以他的生活会像他的诗那么自然，那么不费力。

有人也许会把陶渊明看作"逃避主义者"，然而事实上他并不是。他想要逃避的是政治，而不是生活本身。如果他是逻辑家的话，他也许会决定去做和尚，彻底逃避人生。可是陶渊明是酷爱人生的，他不愿完全逃避人生。在他看来，他的妻儿是太真实了，他的花园，伸过他的庭院的树枝，和他所抚爱的孤松是太可爱了；他因为是一个近情的人，而不是逻辑家，所以他要跟周遭的人物在一起。他就是这样酷爱人生的，他由这种积极的、合理的人生态度而获得他所特有的与生和谐的感觉。这种生之和谐产生了中国最伟大的诗歌。他是尘世所生的，是属于尘世的，所以他的结论不是要逃避人生，而是要"怀良辰以孤往，或植杖而耘耔"。陶渊明仅是回到他的田园和他的家庭的怀抱里去，结果是和谐而不是叛逆。

 Notes

1. 本篇节选改编自林语堂的《人生的盛宴》。
2. 林语堂，中国当代著名学者、文学家、语言学家。早年留学国外，回国后在北京大学等著名大学任教，1966年定居台湾，一生著述颇丰。

Word Bank

混合	merge	中庸哲学	philosophy of the "half-and-half"
和谐的	harmonious	徒劳，无用的	futile
全面的，完美的	well-rounded	尘世的	worldly
道家的	Taoistic	儒家思想	Confucianism
傲慢，自大	arrogance	逃避主义者	escapist
爱抚，抚弄	fondle	叛逆	rebellion

Directions: Please summarize the passage in English. Your summary should be about 150—200 words.

Passage B

Henry David Thoreau

Amanda Davis, Jim Cocola, John Henriksen

Amateur naturalist, essayist, lover of solitude, and poet. Thoreau was a student and follower of the great American philosopher and essayist Ralph Waldo Emerson, and his construction of a hut on Emerson's land at Walden Pond is a fitting symbol of the intellectual debt that Thoreau owed to Emerson. Strongly influenced by Transcendentalism, Thoreau believed in the perfectibility of mankind through education, self-exploration, and spiritual awareness. This view dominates almost all of Thoreau's writing, even the most mundane and trivial, so that even woodchucks and ants take on allegorical meaning. A former teacher, Thoreau's didactic impulse transforms a work that begins as economic reflection and nature writing to something that ends far more like a sermon. Although he values poverty theoretically, he seems a bit of a snob when talking with actual poor people. His style underscores this point, since his writing is full of classical references and snippets of poetry that the educated would grasp but the underprivileged would not.

Confucius, a Chinese sage of the sixth century B.C., known for his sayings and parables collected under the title *Analects*, had a significant effect on the Transcendentalist movement, and was one of Thoreau's favorite authors. Mencius, another Chinese sage of the fourth century B.C. and a disciple of Confucius, whose anthology of sayings and stories collected under the title *The Book of Mencius*, best known for his combination of respect for social harmony and the inward reconciliation with the universe also exerted a powerful influence on Thoreau.

As the foremost American proponent of simple living, Thoreau remains a powerful influence on generation after generation of young freethinkers, but his political importance is more complex than is often thought. It is the liberal side of Thoreau that is most widely remembered today. He sought an absolutely individual stance toward everything, looking for the truth not in social conventions or inherited traditions but only in himself. His casual determination to say "no" to anything he did not care for, or stand for, affirmed and solidified the American model of conscientious objection, a model that resurfaced most notably during the Vietnam War era. His skepticism toward American consumer culture, still in its infancy in the mid-nineteenth century, is even more applicable today than it was in 1847. His willingness to downgrade his lifestyle in return for the satisfactions of self-reliance has set a standard for independent young people for more than a century and a half. It could be argued that Thoreau had significant influence on the profile of American liberalism and of American counterculture.

But Thoreau has a half-hidden conservative side. This schism has led him paradoxically, to be viewed as godfather of both the hippie movement and anti-technology, rural conservatives. His harsh view of the Fitchburg Railway (as he expresses it in the chapter "Sounds") makes modern transportation innovations seem not a boon to his society, but rather a demonic force that threatens natural harmony. His eulogy of a humble lifestyle does not lead him to solidarity with the working poor or to any sort of community-based feeling: rather, it makes him a bit isolated, strangely distant from his neighbors. Thoreau consistently criticizes neighbors he considers bestial, although he theoretically endorses their simplicity.

Thoreau's literary style is often overshadowed by his political and ideological significance, but it is equally important, and just as innovative and free as his social thought. He is a subtle punster and ironist, as when he describes the sun as "too warm a friend," or when he calls the ability to weave men's trousers a "virtue" (a play on the Latin word vir, which means "man"). He uses poetic devices, such as personification, not in a grandiose poetic manner, but in a casual and easygoing one: when he drags his desk and chair out for housecleaning, he describes them as being happy outdoors and reluctant to go back inside. His richly allusive style is brilliantly combined with a down-home feel, so that Thoreau moves from quoting Confucius to talking about woodchucks without a jolt. This combination of the everyday and the erudite finds echoes in later writers such as E.B. White, who also used a rural setting for his witty meditations on life and human nature. Moreover, we feel that

Thoreau is not an armchair reader of literary classics, but is rather attempting to use his erudition to enrich the life he lives in a practical spirit, as when he describes Alex Therien as "Homeric" right after quoting a passage from Homer's work. Homer is not just an old dead poet to Thoreau, but rather a way of seeing the world around him. Thoreau's style is lyrical in places, allegorical in others, and sometimes both at once, as when the poetic beauty of the "Ponds" chapter becomes a delicate allegory for the purity of the human soul. He is a private and ruminative writer rather than a social one, which explains the almost total absence of dialogue in his writing. Yet his writing has an imposing sense of social purpose, and we are aware that despite his claimed yearning for privacy, Thoreau hungers for a large audience to hear his words. The final chapter of *Walden* almost cease being nature writing, and become a straightforward sermon. A private thinker, Thoreau is also a public preacher, whether or not he admits it.

Notes

1. This passage is adapted from *Today's Most Popular Study Guides: Walden,* published by Spark Publishing in 2002.
2. The book *Today's Most Popular Study Guides: Walden* is one of Sparknotes Literature Guides written by students from Harvard University.

Word Bank

solitude	独居,独处	Transcendentalism	超验主义
perfectibility	可完美性	allegorical	讽喻的;寓言的
sage	圣人	Analects	《论语》
Confucius	孔子	Mencius	孟子
reconciliation	和谐	self-reliance	自助
liberalism	自由主义	counterculture	反主流文化
ideological	意识形态的	ruminative	沉思的
grandiose	宏伟的,堂皇的	erudite	博学的
yearn	渴望	preacher	布道家

Directions: Please summarize the passage in Chinese. Your summary should be about 200—300 words.

Unit 4

ART AND ARCHITECTURE

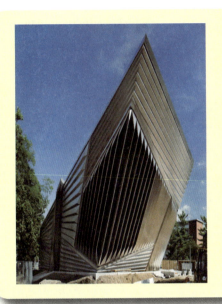

When I say that art is universal, I merely mean that art is not bound to any particular country or to any particular period of time. For art is as old as the human race and it is just as much part of man as are his eyes or his ears or his hunger or his thirst.

—From *The Arts of Mankind* by Hendrik Willem Van Loon

Architecture is produced when a building and a culture come into contact, and connect in such a way that something valuable happens.

—From *Buildings and Culture Produce Architecture*

Learning Objectives

Upon the completion of this unit, you should be able to

Remembering & Understanding	★ read Text A and Text B aloud smoothly with expression indicative of comprehension and tone; ★ identify and explain in your own words the thesis and the major points of Text A and Text B;
Analyzing & Applying	★ use prefix to build new words; ★ make reference to the thesis and/or the major points of Text A and Text B in your writing; ★ produce long, complicated sentences with "as if" clause ;
Evaluating & Creating	★ incorporate instructions in expository paragraphs, ★ reflect on the relationship between culture and architecture; ★ deliver a clear and coherent presentation of your views on some imperishable architecture.

Part One Lead-in

Section 1 Listening: Architecture and Art

Task 1 Filling the Blanks

Directions: Please fill in the blanks with one or two words on the basis of what you have heard.

Architecture is the art of building in which human _____ and construction materials are related so as to furnish practical use as well as an aesthetic solution, thus differing from the pure utility of engineering construction. Architecture can be a structure, a residence, a bridge, a church and a group of buildings. As an art, architecture is _____ abstract and nonrepresentational and involves the _____ of the relationships of spaces, volumes, planes, masses and voids.

The work of _____ influences every aspect of our built environment, from the design of energy efficient buildings to the _____ of new buildings in sensitive contexts. Because of their ability to design and their extensive knowledge of construction, architects' skills are in demand in all areas of property, construction and design. Architects' _____ is invaluable when we need to conserve old buildings, redevelop parts of our towns and cities, understand the impact of a development on a local community, manage a construction program or need advice on the use and _____ of an existing building. Architects work closely with other members of the construction industry including engineers, builders, surveyors, local authority planners and building control officers. Much of their time will be spent visiting sites, assessing the _____ of a project, inspecting building work or managing the construction process. They will also spend time researching old records and drawings, and testing new ideas and construction techniques. Society looks to architects to define new ways of living and working, to develop _____ ways of using existing buildings and creating new ones. We need architects' understanding of the complex process of design and construction to build socially and ecologically _____ cities and communities. Architects can be extremely influential as well as being admired for their imagination and creative skills.

Task 2 Group Discussion

Directions: Please discuss the following questions in pairs or groups based on what you have heard.

1. What is the speaker's understanding of architecture?
2. Why are architects important to a society?
3. Can you talk about some famous architecture?

Section 2 Watching: The Chinese Temples Architecture

Task 1 Group Discussion

Directions: Please watch the video clip "The Chinese Temples Architecture" and discuss the three questions below in pairs or groups.

1. What are the typical characteristics of Chinese temple architecture?
2. Can you show any examples of the influence of Buddhism in China?

Unit 4

3. Name some famous temples in China or around the world.

Task 2 Summarizing

Directions: Please watch the video again, and try to summarize it in 100 words.

Part Two Reading and Writing

Text A

Art Is Universal
Hendrik van Loon

1 Upon that much we can probably agree without any further argument. But when I say, "Art is universal," there is an immediate danger that you will think of art (of either music or painting or *sculpture* or dancing) as if it were some sort of universal language, understood by everybody in every part of the world.

2 Which of course is not true at all. What happens to be the most *sublime* form of music to me, who am sitting at my desk upstairs—say Bach's *Fugue*（赋格曲）in G minor—is just so much unpleasant noise to my poor wife, who within a few minutes will be copying these pages downstairs, far *removed from* the gramophone and the *fiddle*.

3 A *portrait* by Frans Hals or Rembrandt, which makes me hold my breath (for it seems *incredible* that anyone of mere *flesh and blood* could have said quite so much with the help of only a few pigments（颜料）, some oil, a piece of *canvas*, and an old brush)—that same portrait may strike the next visitor as *nothing more than* an unpleasant *combination* of rather drab colors.

4 When I was young, an uncle of mine *incurred* the sincere disapprobation of his *eminently respectable* neighbors because he had brought himself a small sketch by that regrettable social outcast（被抛弃的人）, Vincent van Gogh. Last winter in New York City they had to *call out* the police to keep order among the crowds that were *storming* the museum in which a few of the works of that selfsame Vincent van Gogh were being shown to the public of America.

5 It took us hundreds of years to learn that Chinese painting is in every way as sound and interesting as our own, if not a great deal better.

6 The music of Johann Sebastian Bach was a matter of constant *irritation* to his employers in Leipzig. The Emperor Joseph II of Austria complained to Herr Mozart that there were "too many notes" in his music. Richard Wagner's *compositions* were hooted off（用喊叫轰走）the concert platform. Arab or Chinese music, that makes the average Arab or Chinese roll his eyes in deep rapture, happens to affect me personally

as if I were listening to a *bitterly* contested cat fight in the neighbor's back yard.

7 Wherefore（因此）, when I say that art is universal, I merely mean that art *is not bound to* any particular country or to any particular period of time. For art is as old as the human race and it is just as much part of man as are his eyes or his ears or his hunger or his thirst. The lowest *savage* of the most *desolate* part of Australia, who in a great many ways is quite inferior to the animals which share his loneliness, who has never even learned how to build himself a house or how to wear clothes, had developed a very interesting art of his own. And while we have discovered several groups of natives who have no *conception* whatsoever of religion, we have never, as far as I know, *come across* a race (no matter how far it happened to be removed from the center of civilization) that was completely without some form of artistic expression.

8 That is what I meant a few moments ago when I said that art is universal. And if that be true, it does not really matter very much whether my first chapter starts in Europe or in China, among the Maoris or among the Eskimos. But *in connection with* this, I would like to tell you a story which I found in an old Chinese *manuscript*, or rather in a translation of an old Chinese manuscript, for alas, the language that is spoken by all these millions of people is a closed book to me, and I am too old now to learn it.

9 I went through that stage of development myself, for when I was young, the *absurd slogan* of "art *for* art's *sake*" was still very popular among those who were supposed to know about such things. But that was thirty years ago and since then I am happy to say we have learned better. Today we know that the man who *conceived* the old Brooklyn Bridge was quite as great an artist in his own way as the unknown stonemason who *drew up* the plans for the *cathedral* at Chartres, and most of us can now get just as much real enjoyment out of the perfection of Fred Astaire's dancing as out of the quintet（五重奏）in the last act of the Meistersinger.

10 Let me make myself quite clear, for this is the sort of statement that can *lead up to* all sorts of *futile* discussions. Therefore let it be understood that I do not suggest that we could now do without any further Meistersinger quintets as long as we have Mr. Astaire dancing for us. I realize that there is a *vast* difference between tap dancing and singing or painting. But I have found a very simple way to decide what is good and what is bad. I ask myself this question: "What is this person trying to tell me about his inner emotions?" and "Is he succeeding in telling me his story in so convincing a manner that I understand what he is trying to tell me or not?" Having trained myself to apply this standard of perfection to everything that comes within the ken（知识范围）of my personal observation, I find that I have immensely *enlarged* my own powers of understanding and therefore of enjoyment.

11 That is why some of the subjects have been dealt with in great detail while others have been reduced to a few short pages. I do not think, however, that all this has in any way affected my main purpose—to show the universality that *underlies* all the arts, as it underlies all the *manifestations* of our average, everyday human existence.

Unit 4

New Words

sculpture	[ˈskʌlptʃə]	n.	a three-dimensional work of plastic art 雕刻,塑像
sublime	[səˈblaɪm]	a.	of high moral or intellectual value; elevated in nature or style 庄严的,崇高的;雄伟的
fiddle	[ˈfɪdl]	n.	violin 小提琴
portrait	[ˈpɔːtreɪt]	n.	a painting, drawing or photograph of a person, esp. of the head and shoulders 肖像,肖像画
incredible	[ɪnˈkredɪb(ə)l]	a.	beyond belief or understanding 难以置信的,不可思议的
canvas	[ˈkænvəs]	n.	a strong heavy rough material used for making tents, sails, etc. and by artists for painting on 画布,帆布
combination	[ˌkɒmbɪˈneɪʃn]	n.	two or more things joined or mixed together to form a single unit 接合,联合体
incur	[ɪnˈkɜː]	v.	make oneself subject to; bring upon oneself; become liable to 招致,遭受
eminently	[ˈemɪnəntli]	ad.	(used to emphasize a positive quality) very; extremely 不寻常地,突出地
respectable	[rɪˈspektəb(ə)l]	a.	characterized by proper behavior or conventional conduct; worthy of respect 体面的;可敬的
storm	[stɔːm]	v.	attack a place suddenly 突然冲击,袭击
irritation	[ɪrɪˈteɪʃn]	n.	the psychological state of being irritated or annoyed 激怒,惹恼
composition	[ˌkɒmpəˈzɪʃn]	n.	a piece of music or art, or a poem 作曲,创作
bitterly	[ˈbɪtəli]	ad.	(describing unpleasant or sad feelings) extremely 极为,非常
savage	[ˈsævɪdʒ]	n.	a member of an uncivilized people 野人,野蛮的人
desolate	[ˈdes(ə)lət]	a.	(of a place) empty and without people, making one feels sad or frightened 荒凉的,荒废的
conception	[kənˈsepʃn]	n.	an understanding or a belief of what sth. is or what sth. should be 概念,观念,想法
manuscript	[ˈmænjʊskrɪpt]	n.	the form of a literary work submitted for publication 手稿,底稿,原稿
absurd	[əbˈsɜːd]	a.	inconsistent with reason or logic or common sense 荒谬的,荒唐的,无理性的
slogan	[ˈsləʊɡən]	n.	a word of phrase that is easy to remember to attract people's attention or to suggest an idea quickly 标语,口号
conceive	[kənˈsiːv]	v.	form an idea, plan, etc. in one's mind 构思,设想,考虑
cathedral	[kəˈθiːdr(ə)l]	n.	the main church of a district, under the care of a bishop 大教堂,总教堂

65

futile	[ˈfjuːtaɪl]	a.	producing no result or effect 无效的，无用的
vast	[vɑːst]	a.	extremely large in area, size, amount, etc. 巨大的，广阔的
enlarge	[ɪnˈlɑːdʒ]	v.	become larger or make sth. larger 变大，扩大
underlie	[ˌʌndəˈlaɪ]	v.	be or form the base or cause of sth. 构成……的基础（或起因）
manifestation	[ˌmænɪfeˈsteɪʃ(ə)n]	n.	an event, action or thing that is a sign that sth. exists or is happening 表现，显现

Phrases & Expressions

be removed from	be disconnected with 与……远离
flesh and blood	(used to mean) a normal human with needs, emotions and weaknesses 凡人，普通人
nothing more than	only; just 仅仅，只不过
call out	ask sb. to come, esp. to an emergency 召集，请求……出动
be bound to	be destined to happen 必然；一定要
come across	meet or find sb. or sth. by chance 偶然遇见
in connection with	for reasons connected with sb. or sth. 与……有关
for one's (own) sake	because of the interest or value sth. has, not because of the advantages it may bring 为了……本身的缘故
draw up	make up plans or basic details for sth. 草拟，起草
lead up to	be an introduction to or the cause of sth. 导致；作为……的准备

Notes

1. The text is adapted from the book *The Arts of Mankind* published by Central Compilation & Translation Press in 2011.
2. Hendrik Willem van Loon (1882—1944) was a Dutch-American historian, journalist, and award-winning children's book author. From the 1910s until his death, Van Loon wrote many books, illustrating them himself. Most widely known among these is *The Story of Mankind*, a history of the world especially for children, which won the first Newbery Medal in 1922. However, He also wrote many other very popular books aimed at young adults. As a writer he was known for emphasizing crucial historical events and giving a complete picture of individual characters, as well as the role of the arts in history. He also had an informal and thought-provoking style which, particularly in *The Story of Mankind*, included personal anecdotes.
3. Johann Sebastian Bach (1685—1750) was a German composer and musician of the Baroque period. He enriched established German styles through his skill in counterpoint, harmonic

and motivic organisation, and the adaptation of rhythms, forms, and textures from abroad, particularly from Italy and France. Bach's compositions include the *Brandenburg Concertos, the Goldberg Variations, the Mass in B minor, two Passions,* and over 300 sacred cantatas of which 190 survive. His music is revered for its technical command, artistic beauty, and intellectual depth.

4. Frans Hals the Elder (1582—1666) was a Dutch Golden Age portrait painter who lived and worked in Haarlem, though he was born in the Southern Netherlands (present-day Belgium). He is notable for his loose painterly brushwork, and he helped introduce this lively style of painting into Dutch art. Hals played an important role in the evolution of 17th-century group portraiture.

5. Rembrandt Harmenszoon van Rijn (1606—1669) was a Dutch painter and etcher. He is generally considered one of the greatest painters and printmakers in European art and the most important in Dutch history. His contributions to art came in a period of great wealth and cultural achievement that historians call the Dutch Golden Age when Dutch Golden Age painting, although in many ways antithetical to the Baroque style that dominated Europe, was extremely prolific and innovative, and gave rise to important new genres in painting.

6. Vincent Willem van Gogh (1853—1890), a Dutch artist, was a major Post-Impressionist painter. His work is notable for its rough beauty, emotional honesty, and bold color, which had a far-reaching influence on 20th-century art. After years of painful anxiety and frequent bouts of mental illness, he died aged 37 from a gunshot wound, generally accepted to be self-inflicted (although no gun was ever found).

7. Wolfgang Amadeus Mozart (1756—1791) was a prolific and influential composer of the Classical era. He composed over 600 works, many acknowledged as pinnacles of symphonic, concertante, chamber, operatic, and choral music. He is among the most enduringly popular of classical composers, and his influence on subsequent Western art music is profound; Ludwig van Beethoven composed his own early works in the shadow of Mozart, and Joseph Haydn wrote that "posterity will not see such a talent again in 100 years."

8. Chartres Cathedral (French: Basilique Cathédrale Notre-Dame de Chartres), is a medieval Catholic cathedral of the Latin Church located in Chartres, France, about 80 kilometers southwest of Paris. It is considered one of the finest examples of French Gothic architecture and is a UNESCO World Heritage Site. The current cathedral, mostly constructed between 1194 and 1250, is the last of at least five which have occupied the site since the town became a bishopric in the 4th century.

9. Fred Astaire (1899—1987) was an American dancer, choreographer, singer, musician and actor.

10. *Die Meistersinger von Nürnberg* is a music drama (or opera) in three acts, written and composed by Richard Wagner. It is among the longest operas still commonly performed today, usually taking around four and a half hours.

Task 1　Generating the Outline

Directions: Please identify the thesis of the passage and the main point of each paragraph and find out how these points develop the thesis. You may use the table below to help you.

Para. 7: The thesis	Art is not bound to _____ or _____ because art started from _____ and showed its existence in _____.
Para. 1: The introduction	The author holds the idea that "Art is universal" does not mean _____.
Para. 2: The example	The same music may be _____ to one person or _____ to another.
Para. 3: The example	The understanding of the same painting might _____.
Para. 4: The example	The same art style could not be appreciated until _____.
Para. 5: The example	It may take a very long time for people to understand the arts from _____.
Para. 6: The example	Music styles could be _____ for many people at the very beginning or for people from _____.
Para. 8: The consequence	Arts from different cultures or races are _____.
Para. 9: The consequence	_____ pleasure and satisfaction could be derived from _____ forms of art.
Para. 10: The explanation	The simple way to enlarge the power of understanding and enjoyment is to _____.
Para. 11: The conclusion	I want to show the _____ that form _____ and _____.

Task 2　Understanding the Text

Directions: Please answer the following ten questions based on Text A.

1. Why does the author give the example of Bach's Fugue?
2. What does the author think of the portrait by Rembrandt?
3. What does the popularity of the works of Vincent van Gogh illustrate?
4. How could western people possibly view Chinese painting hundreds of years ago?
5. What does the author really mean when he says "Art is Universal"?
6. How do you understand "a closed book" in the last sentence of Paragraph 8?
7. Why does the author think the slogan "art for art's sake" is absurd?
8. What do different sorts of arts have in common according to the author?
9. What is the standard of perfection related to art according to the author?
10. What is the universality that underlies all the arts?

Unit 4

Task 3 Vocabulary Building

Directions: The prefix en- can be added to adjectives, nouns or other verbs to form new verbs with the meaning of "make" or "become". Now study the following words in the box and complete the six sentences with them. Change the form where necessary.

endanger	enlighten	enforce
ensure	encircle	endear

1. Mrs. Clark came; she sat down on the edge of her patient's bed, and allowed the skinny arms to _____ her.
2. Unlike the IMF, the WTO can _____ its decisions by authorizing trade sanctions.
3. Through the analysis of the major points and the thinking mode of the American enterprise culture, this paper aims to _____ the construction of Chinese enterprise culture.
4. The government said they would try to _____ that old age pension kept up with the ever-increasing cost of living.
5. Doing your share of office chores will also _____ you to your boss and colleagues.
6. Heavy metal pollution has become an important factor in the soil environment and directly or indirectly _____ human health.

Directions: The prefix under- can be added to verbs, nouns and adjectives to form new verbs, nouns and adjectives with the meaning of "not enough". Now study the following words in the box and complete the six sentences with them. Change the form where necessary.

undergo	underage	underestimate
underweight	underdeveloped	underpay

1. The repair cost almost doubles what I thought it would. I really _____ how much damage was done.
2. The investigation found the two factories have employed 85 _____ workers from secondary schools in Sichuan and Guizhou provinces.
3. Obesity isn't the only thing that can put people at a higher risk for dying—being _____ also increases a person's risk of death, according to a study released by St. Michael's Hospital in Toronto.
4. Measures should be taken for the east to help the west, for cities to help the countryside, and for developed regions to help the _____ areas.
5. The once-heavily polluted lake _____ a massive recovery effort during the last two years.
6. Many people in the factory complained that they were overworked and _____.

Task 4 Learning the Phrases

Directions: Please fill in the blanks of the sentences below with the phrases listed in the box. Change the form if necessary.

flesh and blood	be bound to	come across	call out
draw up	lead up to	nothing more than	
for one's (own) sake	be removed from	in connection with	

1. Tanzanian police on Friday arrested two suspects _____ the killing of six lions near the National Park in northern Tanzania on Thursday
2. I asked him to _____ a list of what they're saying at the meeting.
3. Listening to the cries was more than _____ could stand.
4. *Der Untergang* (*The Downfall*) is a 2004 German film written and produced by Bernd Eichinger. It depicts Hitler's final days _____ his suicide.
5. With my knowledge and experience, I knew any decision I'd made _____ be a sound one.
6. They bravely fought the police _____ to suppress them.
7. The book is aimed to help Chinese students overcome many difficulties which they may _____ in reading.
8. Laziness is _____ the habit of resting before you get tired.
9. Children _____ their parents only in extreme circumstances.
10. Learning _____ is sometimes of no value. You should apply what you have learned.

Task 5 Studying the Sentence Structure
Sentences with subjunctive mood used in "as if" clause.
Sentences from the text
1. But when I say, "Art is universal," there is an immediate danger that you will think of art (of either music or painting or sculpture or dancing) as if it were some sort of universal language, understood by everybody in every part of the world. (Para. 1)
2. Arab or Chinese music, that makes the average Arab or Chinese roll his eyes in deep rapture, happens to affect me personally as if I were listening to a bitterly contested cat fight in the neighbor's back yard. (Para. 6)

Directions: Please follow the examples and create five sentences with subjunctive mood used in "as if" clause on your own.
Tips
Note that when the thing introduced is obviously unreal, the subjunctive mood should be used in the "as if" clause.

1. _____
   _____.
2. _____
   _____.
3. _____
   _____.
4. _____
   _____.
5. _____
   _____.

Unit 4

Task 6 Paraphrasing Difficult Sentences

1. A portrait by Frans Hals or Rembrandt, which makes me hold my breath (for it seems incredible that anyone of mere flesh and blood could have said quite so much with the help of only a few pigments, some oil, a piece of canvas, and an old brush)—that same portrait may strike the next visitor as nothing more than an unpleasant combination of rather drab colors.

   _____
   _____.

2. When I was young, an uncle of mine incurred the sincere disapprobation of his eminently respectable neighbors because he had brought himself a small sketch by that regrettable social outcast, Vincent van Gogh.

   _____
   _____.

3. And while we have discovered several groups of natives who have no conception whatsoever of religion, we have never, as far as I know, come across a race (no matter how far it happened to be removed from the center of civilization) that was completely without some form of artistic expression.

   _____
   _____.

4. Therefore let it be understood that I do not suggest that we could now do without any further Meistersinger quintets as long as we have Mr. Astaire dancing for us.

   _____
   _____.

5. Having trained myself to apply this standard of perfection to everything that comes within the ken of my personal observation, I find that I have immensely enlarged my own powers of understanding and therefore of enjoyment.

   _____
   _____.

Task 7 Summarizing the Text

Directions: Please summarize Text A in 150 words. You may use the table in Task 1 to help you.

Task 8 Writing with Instructions

Directions: Write a passage of exposition to instruct foreigners to practile Chinese calligraphy. You should list the things to be done as a helpful instruction. Your writing should be about 200 words. You may use what it provided in the box below to help you.

Tips

1. Exposition is perhaps the type of writing that is most frequently used by a student, a scientist, or a professional. Exposition means expounding or explaining. An expository paper explains or explores something, such as the instruction of making a machine, the causes of a natural or social phenomenon, the planning of a project, or the solution of a problem.

2. When things are explained by instructions, the most important thing in writing is clarity. Ornamental and

ambiguous expressions should be avoided. Secondly, the instructions should be shown in a logical order. Finally, the use of transition words such as *first, next, when, after* and *finally* is very helpful to indicate order or steps.

> To write Chinese calligraphy well, there are some preparations and tips to help the practice. Firstly, [...]

Part Three Reading and Speaking

Text B

Buildings and Culture Produce Architecture
Andrew Ballantyne

1   Buildings can be the most expensive things that civilizations produce. They can absorb any amount of effort and money if they are to compete with the great buildings of *rivals*, and of the past. It might seem misguided to try to outdo（胜过）others when the costs are so high, but no one remembers the civilizations that took such a decision, at least not in architectural history. *By contrast* civilizations such as ancient Egypt and Rome, which built *extravagantly*, seem unavoidable. The imperishable（不朽的）buildings seem to go hand in hand with an imperishable *reputation*, which has always been the appeal of monuments for the powerful. When enough time has passed, all human achievements can seem *fragile*, and Shelley's famous poem Ozymandias shows both the attraction of the monumental and also how delusory（困惑的）its promise of *everlasting* glow can be. One of the things that matters about architecture is how it gives us clues to what really mattered to rulers of the past. Another thing is how it makes it possible for us, the living, to live in certain ways, and to *demonstrate* to each other and ourselves what it is that we really care about, as individuals and as a society. Different civilizations strike different balances between what seems to be owed to the living, and going beyond immediate needs in order to make things that build a reputation in posterity（后世）.

2   Buildings keep us warm and dry and are closely involved in the practicalities of living, but "architecture" always has a cultural *dimension* to it, if we choose to pay attention to it. One of the things that make buildings particularly interesting to archaeologists is that they *are caught up in* so many aspects of life. The way they are organized tells us something about the way people *interact* in them, if we can work out which groups of people are brought together, and which kept apart. The materials from which buildings are made, and the way the materials are handled, can also tell

us a great deal. If the stone came from a long way away, then we know that either there was all efficient transport system or that the stones were very special and worth a great deal of effort. If a building has a steel frame, then we know that it belongs to the modern age because the ancient world didn't know about them. Buildings are an important part of the evidence available to us in knowing about what went on in the distant past, and they also tell us a good deal about what we really care about now. If we, as a society, allow motorways to be built across the countryside, then it can only happen because our care for the countryside is less than our desire to travel conveniently. As individuals we might have made a different decision, but as a society, given the flows and concentrations of money that *circulate*, and given the political processes that *mediate* the decisions, the buildings that surround us are produced. As individuals, most of us can do very little to shape the built environment in general. In some *circumstances*, though, concentrations of wealth and power have made it possible for individuals to command great changes. Buildings can be beautiful and inspiring, but if they are built (rather than just imagined) then they always have an economic and political aspect, as well as an *aesthetic* aspect. There are other aspects too, such as the technical side of things. Will it stand up? Will it keep the rain out? Can it be kept warm? Will it overheat? Can I use it as a place where I can live the life I want? Do I want to be the sort of person who lives in a place like this?

3   Given that a building has all these aspects, it is possible to write about architecture in ways that *bring* one or another of them *to the fore*. A history of building technology would be one possibility. This would be a story of progress, as more technically *sophisticated* ways of building superseded（取代）the more primitive ones. There would be significant advances, like the introduction of cement, and the arch, and a demonstration of the new types of building that these *innovations* made possible. What we *lose sight of* in this particular *narrative* is the fact that, at a given time, it is likely that few buildings will be technically advanced. Most buildings are just ordinary, and do not fall down or stop being useful the moment a technical advance has been made. Just as many people in Europe live in houses that were built a hundred years or more ago.

4   We like to think that the canonic（按照教规的）buildings have timeless value that sails *serenely* across the vagaries（奇想）of human histories, but on closer examination this view cannot be *sustained*. There is no doubt that some buildings have always been valued, but they are valued in different ways at different times. It would be *idiotic* to argue that the Parthenon, for example, had no great value, but it has been valued at different times because it seemed to express different things, such as the *triumph* of Athens over her *adversaries*, or as a symbol of the roots of democracy. The value remains high, but it is *volatile*. Buildings are solid things, and the properties that they have are *inherent* in them. Architecture is produced when a building and a culture *come into contact,* and connect in such a way that something valuable happens. We might be thrilled by it, or calmed, feel challenged or charmed, but if we do not pay attention to

those responses and cultivate them, then architecture dies in us, and the built world is an *arid* place. But once one knows something about architecture then buildings *come alive*, and it is possible to see unconscious expressions of skill and intelligence at work wherever one goes, possibly set alongside expressions of *vanity,* greed, and incompetence. We like to see the great buildings around the world as the clearest expressions of one lofty ideal or another. We see them as something imperishable that *embodies* a *fleeting* glimpse of eternity, and we will travel across the world to encounter them. But there are also pleasures closer to home, which may be no less intense, involving a feeling of rapport with a place, which may involve a surprising range of the *contradictory* emotions involved in any long-term relationship.

New Words

rival	[ˈraɪvl]	n.	a person, company or thing that competes with another in sport, business, etc. 对手,竞争者
extravagantly	[ɪkˈstrævəgəntlɪ]	ad.	in an abundant or wasteful manner 过分地,铺张地,挥霍无度地
reputation	[ˌrepjuˈteɪʃn]	n.	the opinion that people have about what sb. or sth. is like, based on what has happened in the past 名声,名气
fragile	[ˈfrædʒl]	a.	easily broken or damaged or destroyed 易碎的,脆弱的,虚弱的
everlasting	[ˌevəˈlɑːstɪŋ]	a.	continuing for ever; never change 永久的,永恒的
demonstrate	[ˈdemənˌstret]	v.	show or demonstrate something to an interested audience 表明,显示,演示
dimension	[daɪˈmenʃən]	n.	the magnitude of something in a particular direction (esp. length or width or height) 尺寸,维度
interact	[ˌɪntərˈækt]	v.	act together or towards others or with others 相互作用,相互影响
circulate	[ˈsɜːrkjəleɪt]	v.	become widely known and passed on; cause to become widely known 传递,循环,流通
mediate	[ˈmiːdieɪt]	v.	succeed in finding a solution to a disagreement between people or groups 经调解解决
circumstance	[ˈsɜːkəmstəns]	n.	(usually pl.) the conditions and facts that are connected with affect a event or an action 环境,情况

Unit 4

aesthetic	[iːsˈθetɪk]	a.	concerned with beauty and art and the understanding of beautiful things 美学的,审美的
sophisticated	[səˈfɪstɪkeɪtɪd]	a.	(of a machine, system, etc.) clever and complicated in the way that it works or is presented 复杂的,精致的
innovation	[ˌɪnəˈveɪʃn]	n.	a creation (a new device or process) resulting from study and experimentation 改革,创新,革新
narrative	[ˈnærətɪv]	n.	a description of events, esp. in a novel 叙事,叙述
serenely	[səˈriːnlɪ]	ad.	in a calm and peacefully manner 安详地,宁静地
sustain	[səˈsteɪn]	v.	make sth. continue for some time without becoming less 维持,持续
idiotic	[ˌɪdiˈɒtɪk]	a.	very stupid or silly 白痴的,愚蠢的
triumph	[ˈtraɪʌmf]	n.	(over) a great success, achievement or victory 大胜,凯旋,巨大的成就
adversary	[ˈædvəsəri]	n.	a person that sb. is opposed to and competing with in an argument or a battle 对手,敌手
volatile	[ˈvɒlətaɪl]	a.	tending to vary often or widely 易变的,不稳定的
inherent	[ɪnˈhɪərənt]	a.	being a basic of permanent part of sb. or sth. and that cannot be removed 内在的,天生的,固有的
arid	[ˈærɪd]	a.	with nothing new or interesting in it 枯燥无味的,无趣的
vanity	[ˈvænəti]	n.	feelings of excessive pride 虚荣,虚荣心
embody	[ɪmˈbɒdi]	v.	express or represent an idea or a quality 体现,表现,象征
fleeting	[ˈfliːtɪŋ]	a.	lasting for a markedly brief time 飞逝的,短暂的,稍纵即逝的
contradictory	[ˌkɒntrəˈdɪktəri]	a.	containing or showing a contradiction 矛盾的,对立的

Phrases & Expressions

by contrast	showing a very different situation from the one mentioned before 对比,对照
be caught up in	to be involved in sth. usually unwillingly 被卷入,牵涉,涉及
bring sth. to the fore	to make sth. become noticed by people 使……处于显要地位
lose sight of	to stop considering sth.; to forget sth. 忽略,忽视
come into contact	meet with each other 与……联系,遇到
come alive	(of a subject or an event) to become interesting and exciting 活跃起来,栩栩如生

 **Notes**

1. This passage was adapted from *Architecture—A Very Short Introduction* published by Foreign Language Teaching and Research Press in 2013. The book begins by looking at how architecture acquires meaning through tradition, and concludes with the exoticism of avant-garde. Illustrations of particular buildings help to anchor the general points with specific examples, from ancient Egypt to the present day.

2. Andrew Ballantyne qualified and practiced as an architect, and then moved into academic work. He has held research and teaching posts at the universities of Sheffield, Bath, and Newcastle, where he is now Professor of Architecture. He has written on architectural history and theory, and his previous books are *Architecture, Landscape and Liberty* and *What is Architecture?*

3. Percy Bysshe Shelley (1792—1822), one of the most famous British romanticism poets, was born in a noble family in 1792. He entered in Oxford University at 20 years old after his education in Eaton school. In Oxford he became an Atheist. He was dismissed from school for his anti-Christ Philosophical Essays. Thenceforth, he wrote many poems to incite people's revolution and Irish independence. He was exiled from England and went to Italy. Still, he wrote poems to encourage Italian liberation struggle. One of the master pieces of Shelley is the famous poem *Ode to the West Wind*.

4. The Parthenon is a former temple on the Athenian Acropolis, Greece, dedicated to the goddess Athena, whom the people of Athens considered their patron. Construction began in 447 BC when the Athenian Empire was at the height of its power. It was completed in 438 BC although decoration of the building continued until 432 BC. It is the most important surviving building of Classical Greece, generally considered the zenith of the Doric order. Its decorative sculptures are considered some of the high points of Greek art. The Parthenon is regarded as an enduring symbol of Ancient Greece, Athenian democracy and western civilization, and one of the world's greatest cultural monuments.

Task 1 Summarizing

Directions: Fill in the blanks in the following text outline with key points based on an overall understanding and then make an oral summary.

1. Different civilizations may show different concerns about the construction of buildings. There're two mentioned:

    a. _____

    b. _____

2. Buildings involve many aspects such as:

    a. _____

    b. _____

    c. _____

    d. _____

Unit 4

3. We could have a discussion on architecture by underlining the history of building technology, but the problem of this method is _____.
4. Architecture is the production of the encounter of _____ and _____.

Task 2   Reflecting on the Text

Directions: You have just read Buildings and Culture Produce Architecture. What do you think of the relationship between culture and architecture? Discuss the passage with your partner and then give an oral presentation of your reflection on this passage. You may mention the following points in your discussion.

Guiding Questions:
1. The basic function of buildings
2. Cultural aspects of buildings in different cultures
3. Factors that make buildings imperishable

Task 3   Making a Presentation

Directions: Give an oral presentation of your views on the following topics centering around "culture and architecture". You should state your views clearly.

1. The cultural aspect of buildings could be increasingly appreciated with the passage of time.
2. An ordinary building could also be a mirror of a particular culture.

Below are some words and expressions that you might find useful in your presentation.

1）scheme
2）classicism
3）modernism
4）religious
5）practicability
6）philosophy
7）building materials
8）break out of routine

Part Four   Cross Cultural Communication

Passage A

舞蹈的建筑
刘心武

我曾写过一篇《跃动》，谈及中外建筑设计中追求灵动飞跃意趣的一些例子，现在要进一步探讨：建筑物是否可以呈舞蹈的态势？"建筑是凝固的音乐"已成为人们的共识，建筑与绘画、雕塑、文学、戏剧相通，争议也不大，但建筑能与舞蹈相通吗？初想，答案是否定的。建筑就其功能性而言，首先得稳定，没有坚固不移的品质，就没有安全感，否则人们怎么使用它？但再往细想，音乐其实是比舞蹈更加"非空间"的"纯时间"艺术，没有连续不断的流动，哪来的音乐？但人们拿音乐比喻建筑时，加了一个"凝固"的限制词，就觉得二者在审美上相融通了。那么，在舞蹈与建筑之间也嵌入一个"凝固"的限制词，把某些建筑比喻为"凝固的舞蹈"，可不可以呢？我觉得那也是可以的。

在中国古典建筑与西方古典建筑里，要找出"凝固的舞蹈"的例子来，似乎比较困难。我想这是因为古典时代人们的思路不像如今这么多元狂放，更因为建筑设计手段与施工技术远没有如今这么先进，所以难以"舞动"；如今更有各种新型建筑材料接踵出现，建筑设计师们好比巧妇拥有庞大的米粮库，可以随心所欲地在炊事中大显身手。因此，舞蹈性思维进入了某些建筑设计师大脑，一些"舞蹈的建筑"也便应运而生。这是可喜的事。

最先把舞蹈元素糅进设计中的，可能是某些大型运动场馆的天棚。德国慕尼黑奥运会运动场开风气之先，把天棚设计成仿佛往巨人肩膀后甩去的风衣，呈舞动的态势，生动活泼，奇诡醒目。此种设计后来渐成范式，只是新的设计里不断花样翻新，韩国为世界杯足球赛新建的比赛场，就是最新的一个变体。这种糅进舞蹈元素的设计方式也在世界各地的机场设计中流行开来，美国中部科罗拉多州丹佛空港的天棚就恍如一大匹在风中呈曲波状舞蹈的银缎。舞蹈元素说白了就是大量使用非规整曲线曲面。美籍华裔建筑大师贝聿铭的建筑设计里使用非规整曲线与曲面非常谨慎，可以说是"惜曲如金"，但他为台湾东海大学设计的鲁斯教堂，用四片从地面升起在顶处合拢携抱的略微呈扭动感的曲面墙体构成，却营造出了一种端庄而又轻盈的舞姿感，非常符合"年轻人的教堂"这样的功能要求。

但是，如果不仅仅是糅进舞蹈元素，而是完全地"舞蹈化"，这样的建筑是可能的吗？回答是肯定的。美国建筑师盖里就为西班牙毕尔巴鄂市的古根海姆博物馆做出了这样的设计。他所设计的这座博物馆几乎完全由"扭动的肢体"构成，没有一个立面是规整的，不仅天棚，所有的使用空间，包括走廊，充满了舞蹈的曲面和曲线。建成后的博物馆，通体仿佛是几个穿着紧身衣的舞蹈家在忘情的舞动中绞缠在一起。他自己说，如果没有电脑，拿以往的设计工具是不可能做出这样的设计的。施工过程中，他亲自在工地参与，也深感用传统工艺和传统材料是无法兑现他的设计的。这座博物馆已于1997年建成开放，成为该市甚至全西班牙的新地标。当然，争议也是有的，一是认为太怪异，二是批评其造价太高。毕尔巴鄂古根海姆博物馆在地球上的出现，是建筑艺术的新胜利，但这种"舞蹈的建筑"恐怕只能作为一种流派，而且是小流派而存在。这一流派的设计，尤其是化为大地上的实际存在，需要天时、地利、人和各方面因素的机缘凑迫。但特别看重建筑设计的艺术创造内涵的中国建筑师，尤其是年青一代，据我所知，有的一直在寻找机会施展自己的"舞蹈性思维"。中国传统艺术里，跟舞蹈最相通的领域是书法里的狂草，舞剑器与挥毫墨绝对是异曲同工，中国建筑师在借鉴舞蹈时也借鉴书法，这构成一种创新优势，是特别可贵的。赵波就设计出了若干从中国书法笔意演化出的综合性楼体，尽管到目前为止这种设计只是一种观念性的展示，尚无被业主采用的可能，而且就我所见到的几个图形而言，还不免有些个生硬，但这种创新的设计思维，却是应该被大力肯定的。中国什么时候能出现"舞蹈的建筑"？不着急，早晚会出现的吧。

Notes

1. 本篇节选改编自林木编选的新课标语文同步读本(初中卷)"山水的圣谕"。(山东人民出版社，2011)
2. 刘心武，1942年6月4日出生，中国当代著名作家、红学研究家。笔名刘浏、赵壮汉等。其作品以关注现实为特征，以《班主任》闻名文坛，长篇小说《钟鼓楼》获得茅盾文学奖。20世纪90年代后，成为《红楼梦》的积极研究者，曾在中央电视台《百家讲坛》栏目进行系列讲座，对红学在民间的普及与发展起到促进作用。

Unit 4

Word Bank

凝固的	frozen	糅进	be mixed into
争议	dispute	范式	paradigm
比喻	metaphor	立面	vertical surface
多元	diverse/ pluralistic	曲面	curved surface
狂放	unrestrained	曲线	curve
设计手段	designing method	流派	genre
施工技术	construction technique	书法	calligraphy
建筑材料	building materials	借鉴	borrow...from

Directions: Please summarize the passage in English. Your summary should be about 150—200 words.

Passage B

Hagia Sophia

David Watkin

The greatest of Justinian's churches was the Hagia Sophia (the church of the Holy Wisdom of God), in Constantinople (Istanbul). The church which it replaced, founded in the Nika Insurrections of 532. Justianian suppressed these riots and took the opportunity of making his victory by erecting in 532—537 the Hagia Sophia, one of the largest, most lavish and most expensive buildings of all time. His architects were two skilled scientists and mathematicians from Asia Minor, Anthemios of Tralles and Isidorus of Miletus. The fact that they were partly account for the fresh approach which enabled them to design an unprecedented domed structure.

The plan consists of a huge rectangle measuring 230 by 250 feet (71×77m) enclosing a central square space defined by four piers carrying a dome so vast that it dominates the whole interior, though as originally constructed the dome was some 20 feet (6m) lower than the present one. Unlike the dome of the Pantheon which, after the manner of an outside igloo, was supported in a structurally unimaginative way on the 20-foot thick walls of a hollow drum, the dome Hagia Sophia surmounted a square not a circular space, and was supported on pendentives rising from the piers. This method of constructing a dome, which may have originated in Persia through it had not been used on this scale before, meant that it was possible to dispense with the supporting walls beneath it. The square below the dome could thus be opened out into further spaces surrounding it on all four sides, as at Hagia Sophia. Here the central space is separated from galleried aisles on the north and south sides by dramatic two-storeyed screens of marble columns carrying arches, while on the east and west sides there are no subsidiary supports at all, so that the space flows uninterruptedly into the area beneath the two huge semi-domes which about on to the east and west ends of the central dome. These semi-domes, of the same diameter (107 feet; 32.5m) as the principal dome, the thrust of which they help support, are themselves extended into lower semi-circular apses or conches.

The result is that through the whole structure is rationally and symmetrically organized it appears mysterious, for our eyes are continually led from one space to another whose precise extent and form we are unable to ascertain. The poetic ambiguity of this flickering contrast of light and shade is reflected in miniature in the characteristic capital which crowns the Byzantine column. Whereas in Roman Corinthian capitals and acanthus foliage sprang unequivocally from the solid bell, the bell of Byzantine capital was masked by an intricately spiky overall foliage carving, undercut by drilling so that it resembled a kind of starched lacy veil.

It is tempting to try to relate the interior to the liturgy for which it was designed, and even to see the former as a necessary consequence or expression of the latter. However, the architectural historian is on difficult ground here because little is known with certainty about the services and the use of the churches in sixth-century Constantinople. It has sometimes been claimed, on the basis of much later Byzantine usages, that mystery and concealment were essential to the early liturgy. According to this view, the nave or central space was reserved for the clergy while the ordinary congregation caught glimpsed of the splendid ceremonies from the aisles and galleries. This would then be one reason why the centrally-planned church was adopted for the Eastern liturgy, since the attempt to provide adequate space for the clergy in the basilican plan produced a choir encroaching into a nave which, as at S. Clemente, would have looked better without this encumberment. It has also been suggested, and equally vigorously denied, that curtains in the aisles and sanctuary further concealed the Sacrifice of the Mass from the lay congregation. What we know with certainty is that at the beginning of Mass in Hagia Sophia the patriarch leading his clergy and, on state occasions, the emperor leading his court would go in procession into the nave. The patriarch would emerge from the sanctuary after the Consecration, the most solemn moment of the Mass, in order to exchange the Kiss of Peace with the emperor. This sacred sealing of the divine pact between God, church and state took place in public view below the eastern rim of the great central dome which was itself a tangible symbol of the Dome of Heaven.

This earthly image of the celestial hierarchy was constructed throughout not with the heavy brick-faced concrete of Roman imperial architecture, but with thin bricks, except for the ashlar blocks which comprised the eight main piers. The light bricks were used to create a series of domes like diaphanous bubbles, an effect which led Procopius to describe the upper parts of the building as "hanging in mid-air." The experiment turned out to be too hazardous, for the shallow brick dome collapsed in 558 and was replaced by the ribbed dome of steeper pitch which, extensively repaired, survives today. The walls inside were covered with a shimmering skin of the colored marbles, porphyry and basalt in which the Empire was so rich, while the vault and domes were sheathed in mosaic composed of glass and semi-precious stones which glimmered in the light of sun and especially of the numerous gold lamps, candlesticks and chandeliers.

1. This passage is adapted from the fourth edition of *A History of Western Architecture* published by Laurence King Publishing in 2005.
2. David Watkin is Emeritus Professor of the History of Architecture at the University of Cambridge and a Fellow of Peterhouse. He has written many books, among them are *Morality and Architecture Revisited* and *Sir John Soane*(1996), and is a leading authority on Classicism and its successive renewals in architecture.

Unit 4

Word Bank

Justinian	查士丁尼一世(东罗马帝国皇帝)	marble column	大理石柱
Holy Wisdom of God	上帝圣智	Byzantine	拜占庭风格的
insurrection	暴动,叛乱	foliage	树叶
suppress	压制,镇压	lacy veil	蕾丝面纱
lavish	浪费的,挥霍的	liturgy	礼拜仪式
dome	圆屋顶	clergy	牧师,教士
rectangle	长方形	congregation	会众,集会
pier	墩,窗间壁	patriarch	元老,族长
igloo	圆顶建筑	celestial hierarchy	(宗教)天阶等级
surmount	战胜,克服	diaphanous	半透明的
pendentive	穹隅,帆拱	porphyry	斑岩
aisle	过道	basalt	玄武岩

Directions: Please summarize the passage in Chinese. Your summary should be about 200—300 words.

Unit 5

DEMOCRACY AND LAW

In the contract entered into by the citizens and the State, the State obligates itself to promote the welfare of the citizens, and to provide a mechanism for changing the law when its "commands are unjust."

—From The State and The Individual

If we wish to be free—if we mean to preserve inviolate those inestimable privileges for which we have been so long contending—if we mean not basely to abandon the noble struggle in which we have been so long engaged, and which we have pledged ourselves never to abandon until the glorious object of our contest shall be obtained—we must fight!

—From Give Liberty or Give Me Death

Learning Objectives

Upon the completion of this unit, you should be able to

Remembering & Understanding	★ read Text A and Text B aloud smoothly with expression indicative of comprehension and tone; ★ identify and explain in your own words the thesis and the major points of Text A and Text B;
Analyzing & Applying	★ make reference to the thesis and/or the major points of Text A and Text B in your writing; ★ produce long, complicated sentences with inverted word order; ★ get some knowledge about the formation of compound adjectives and compound verbs;
Evaluating & Creating	★ produce paragraph(s) by comparison and contrast; ★ give an oral report of your reflection on Text B; ★ deliver a clear and coherent presentation of your views on some topics concerning Text B.

Unit 5

Part One Lead-in

Section 1 Listening: The Founding Principles of American Democracy

Task 1 Fill in the blanks

Directions: Please fill in the blanks with one or two words on the basis of what you have heard.

American democracy is based on certain founding principles including the principle of majority rule. In a democratic _____ body, decisions are made by voting. In the U. S., voting is not just a tool for selecting political leaders and passing laws. It is also a way of making decisions in the business world, in social groups, in schools, and even within the family. Americans believe that people should take part in making the rules they must _____. American children are introduced to the ideas of majority rule and representative government at a very early age. Many families hold weekly meetings to determine _____ and activities. Most schools have student councils with elected representatives so that students can voice their opinions about school regulations and activities. In the adult world, all kinds of organizations elect officers and make decisions by voting.

"All men are created equal," says *the Declaration of Independence*. This statement does not mean all human beings are equal in ability or _____. It means that all people should be treated equally before the law and given equal _____ and opportunities. Equal opportunity means an equal chance for good education and a good job.

The American _____ to equality of opportunity inspires what is commonly called the American dream — the belief that anyone can achieve success through honesty and hard work. For many _____ Americans, this dream became reality. Financial success has often been the result of taking a risk, of quitting a salaried position and starting one's own new business. Social _____ — movement from one social class to another — has always been characteristic of the U. S.. It is usually achieved by improving one's educational level, _____, and / or income.

Task 2 Group Discussion

Directions: Please discuss the following questions in pairs or groups based on what you have heard.

1. According to the material, what is the core of American democracy?
2. How do you think American democracy helps people realize their American dream?
3. What's your understanding of American democracy?

Section 2 Watching: American Election

Task 1 Group Discussion

Directions: Please watch the video clip "American Election" and discuss the three questions below in pairs or groups.

1. List the most important political parties in the US.
2. How is the President of the US elected?
3. What are the stages of the Great Election?

Task 2 Summarizing

Directions: Please watch the video again, and try to summarize the speaker's main points.

Part Two   Reading and Writing

Text A

The State and the Individual
Arthur J. Minton

1   As a young person grows up, Socrates tells us, he has an *ample* opportunity to *acquaint himself with* the way of life in his community. He observes the customs, traditions, institutional life, the workings of government, and citizens exercising rights and duties. If he finds this offensive, he may go elsewhere, to a place where the surroundings are more suitable and satisfactory in his view. Should he stay, however, he must accept the duties of a citizen as the price of his rights.

2   *Implicitly*, Socrates says, an adult *enters into* a contract with the State which involves these terms: the State promises to protect the individual and to promote his well-being, and, in turn, the individual promises to respect the State and to obey its laws. Should an individual object to a particular law, the contract requires him to obey it until he succeeds in *securing* a change through procedures for that purpose provided in the law. On this basis, Socrates points out that if he were to agree to escape, he would *violate* his promise to obey the law. He was not prepared to *repudiate* his obligation merely because the law had worked to his *detriment* in the case at hand. It would seem, then, for Socrates, that a citizen should obey all of the laws all the time, being neither selective nor inconsistent.

3   The most serious objection to the position of Socrates comes from those who point to the State's enormous potential for evil. History is filled with examples of governments *sanctioning* acts, laws, or policies which are morally *repugnant*. Is a citizen to be obedient to a law which he believes is immoral? To Henry David Thoreau the answer is a decisive and *resounding* "No"! Thoreau lived in America in the nineteenth century, when the government still permitted the owning of slaves. Unless an individual wishes to be guilty of *complicity* in this morally *despicable* practice, he must withdraw his support from government now. It is not enough to wait patiently until enough people oppose slavery to *outlaw* it. Thoreau therefore refused to pay his taxes, fully understanding that the price of his refusal would be jail. When government *condones* evil, he insists, "the true place for a just man is a prison."

4   You should take note of the mode of Thoreau's resistance to government. While he refused to *comply* with a law that was immoral, and to support the government that *perpetuated* such a law, he *stopped short of* violence. For Thoreau one does not create a community of morally sensitive individuals by *bashing* in heads. Not only did he *eschew* violence as a technique, but he readily accepted the penalty which the law provided for its violation to show that his motives were pure. These ideas were adopted both by Mhandas Gandhi, leader of the Indian resistance to British colonial rule, and Dr. Martin Luther King, whose struggle for civil rights cost him his life.

5   Robert Paul Wolff, a *contemporary* philosopher, raises perhaps the most basic question of all: Does the State have the authority to command *obedience* from the citizens, their own moral views *notwithstanding*? To answer this question he *reflects on* what it means to be a moral agent. A moral agent, he says, must be "*autonomous*," thinking and judging for himself, and accepting responsibility for his actions. He may not *relinquish* his *autonomy*, there by permitting others to *dictate* how he should act, and yet remain a moral agent. The obvious implication of this is that the State cannot issue binding commands to individuals. A citizen, therefore, has no duty to obey laws, even though he may decide to obey them for self-interested or *prudential* reasons. Wolff calls this view "philosophical *anarchism*."

6   Much of the literature of resistance grows out of the State's *potential* for evil. Yet the State also has a potential for good. If the State is a *curse*, it is also a *blessing*. Ironically, Wolff himself *hints at* this when he admits that he obeys the law "because of the obvious moral considerations concerning the value of order." Reflect on his words for a moment. Is he not saying that there is a definite moral good for us—order? And is it not the case that the State, by passing and enforcing laws, assures order? If the State is not good in itself—an "intrinsic good," it is perhaps a necessary means to good—an "instrumental good." If this is so, as Socrates would be required many times to obey the law and to support the State.

7   On the other hand, Socrates himself may have opened the door to resistance. In the contract entered into by the citizens and the State, the State *obligate* itself to promote the welfare of the citizens, and to provide a mechanism for changing the law when its "commands are unjust." Now suppose the States *defaults* on its part of the bargain. Suppose it becomes self-serving and tyrannical *at the expense of* the people, or denies them an effective opportunity to change an unjust law. Perhaps then the individual's obligation to obey the law would cease.

8   Thus, while Socrates urges us to obey the law, and emphasizes the state as a blessing, his argument does not necessarily call for blind obedience to any state. Likewise, while Thoreau and Wolff urge us to do the right, and emphasize the state as a curse, they imply that the state can promote moral ends. From these considerations it is obvious that the problem of "law or *conscience*" is very complicated. Try to *formulate* your own position as you read these *landmark* statements on the problem. As you do, you will probably find, as so many have, that "The *speculative* line of *demarcation* where obedience ought to end and resistance must begin, is faint, *obscure*, and not easily *definable*."

ample	[ˈæmpl]	a.	more than enough 充足的
implicitly	[ɪmˈplɪsɪtlɪ]	ad.	without doubting or questioning 毫无疑问地
secure	[səˈkjʊr]	v.	make safe; make certain of 使安全, 确保
violate	[ˈvaɪəleɪt]	v.	break an oath, a treaty, etc. 违反, 违背
repudiate	[rɪˈpjuːdɪeɪt]	v.	refuse to acknowledge, ratify, or recognize as valid 拒绝, 拒付
detriment	[ˈdetrɪmənt]	n.	a damage or loss 损害物, 损伤
sanction	[ˈsæŋkʃn]	v.	give authority or permission to 批准, 支持
repugnant	[rɪˈpʌgnənt]	a.	offensive to the mind 令人厌恶的; 抵触的
resounding	[rɪˈzaʊndɪŋ]	a.	characterized by reverberation 响亮的
complicity	[kəmˈplɪsɪti]	n.	guilt as an accomplice in a crime or offense 合谋; 共犯
despicable	[dɪˈspɪkəbəl]	a.	worthy of only being despised and rejected 可鄙的; 卑鄙的
outlaw	[ˈaʊt͵lɔ]	v.	declare illegal 宣布……为不合法
condone	[kənˈdoʊn]	v.	excuse, overlook or make allowances for 容忍, 宽恕
comply	[kəmˈplaɪ]	v.	(with) act in accordance with someone's rules, commands, or wishes 遵从; 顺从
perpetuate	[pərˈpetʃueɪt]	v.	cause to continue or prevail 使永存; 使不朽
bash	[bæʃ]	v.	strike violently or crushingly 猛打, 重击
eschew	[ɪsˈtʃuː]	v.	avoid and stay away from deliberately; stay clear of 回避, 避开; 戒绝
contemporary	[kənˈtempərəri]	a.	existing, occurring, or living at the same time; of the present time 同时代的; 当代的
obedience	[əˈbiːdɪəns]	n.	the act of obeying; dutiful or submissive behavior with respect to another person 服从; 顺从
notwithstanding	[͵nɑːtwɪθˈstændɪŋ]	ad.	despite anything to the contrary (usually following a concession) 虽然; 尽管
autonomous	[ɔːˈtɑːnəməs]	a.	(of political bodies) not controlled by outside forces; existing as an independent entity 自治的
relinquish	[rɪˈlɪŋkwɪʃ]	v.	part with a possession or right 放弃; 放手
autonomy	[ɔːˈtɑːnəmi]	n.	immunity from arbitrary exercise of authority; political independence 自治; 自主
dictate	[ˈdɪkteɪt]	v.	issue commands or orders for; say out loud for the purpose of recording 支配, 主宰; 口授

Unit 5

prudential	[pruˈdɛnʃəl]	*a.*	arising from or characterized by prudence especially in business matters 谨慎的, 细心的
anarchism	[ˈænərkɪzəm]	*n.*	a political theory favoring the abolition of governments 无政府主义
potential	[pəˈtenʃl]	*n.*	the inherent capacity for coming into being 潜力, 潜能
curse	[kɜːrs]	*n.*	an appeal to some supernatural power to inflict evil on someone or some group; sth. causing misery or death 诅咒; 祸端
blessing	[ˈblesɪŋ]	*n.*	the formal act of approving; sth. good or helpful 祝福; 幸事
obligate	[ˈɒbləˌgeɪt]	*v.*	to make someone to do sth. because it is right, or a duty, etc. 使……负担起义务
default	[dɪˈfɔːlt]	*v.*	on not to do sth. that you are legally supposed to, especially not to pay money you are supposed to pay 不履行; (尤其指)不偿还债务
conscience	[ˈkɑːnʃəns]	*n.*	the part of your mind that tells you what you do is morally right or wrong 良心, 良知
formulate	[ˈfɔːrmjuleɪt]	*v.*	come up with (an idea, plan, explanation, theory, or principle) after a mental effort 构想, 制定
landmark	[ˈlændmɑːrk]	*n.*	an event marking a unique or important historical change of course or one on which important developments depend 里程碑, 地标
speculative	[ˈspekjələtɪv]	*a.*	not based on fact or investigation 推测的, 推理的
demarcation	[ˌdiːmɑːrˈkeɪʃn]	*n.*	the boundary of a specific area 界限
obscure	[əbˈskjʊr]	*a.*	not clearly understood or expressed 晦涩的, 不清楚的
definable	[dɪˈfaɪnəbl]	*n.*	capable of being defined, limited or explained 可定义的, 可确定的

Phrases & Expressions

acquaint oneself with	oneself make sb./oneself familiar with or aware of sth. 使自己熟悉
enter into	be involved in sth. like an agreement, discussion or relationship 订立(协议); 加入(讨论)
stop short of	not to do or say sth. 不再, 停止
reflect on	consider or think carefully about something 考虑; 反思
hint at sth.	suggest or imply indirectly 暗示, 示意
at the expense of	at the cost of or at the sacrifice of 以……为代价

Notes

1. The passage is taken from the article *The State and The Individual*. The writer Arthur J. Minton (1942—) is also the co-author of a philosophy book *Philosophy: Paradox and Discovery*, which presents philosophy as an immediate, vital and challenging process of discovery.

2. Socrates (469—399 B.C.) was a classical Greek philosopher who is credited with laying the fundamentals of modern Western philosophy. He is known for creating Socratic irony and the Socratic method (elenchus). He is best recognized for inventing the teaching practice of pedagogy, wherein a teacher questions a student in a manner that draws out the correct response. He has had a profound influence on Western philosophy, along with his students Plato and Aristotle. Though much of Socrates' contribution is to the field of ethics, his input to the field of epistemology and logic is also noteworthy.

3. Henry David Thoreau (1817—1862) was an American author, poet, philosopher, abolitionist, naturalist, tax resister, development critic, surveyor and historian. A leading transcendentalist, Thoreau is best known for his book *Walden*, a reflection upon simple living in natural surroundings, and his essay *Resistance to Civil Government* (also known as *Civil Disobedience*), an argument for disobedience to an unjust state.

4. Mohandas Gandhi (1869—1948) was the preeminent leader of Indian independence movement in British-ruled India. Employing nonviolent civil disobedience, Gandhi led India to independence and inspired movements for civil rights and freedom across the world. The honorific *Mahatma* which means "high-souled" or "venerable" applied to him first in 1914 in South Africa and is now used worldwide. He is also called Bapu, which means "father" or "papa" in India.

5. Dr. Martin Luther King (1929—1968) was an American Baptist minister, activist, humanitarian, and leader in the African-American Civil Rights Movement. He is best known for his role in the advancement of civil rights using nonviolent civil disobedience based on his Christian beliefs.

6. Robert Paul Wolff (1933—) is a contemporary American political philosopher and professor emeritus at the University of Massachusetts Amherst. Wolff has written widely on many topics in political philosophy such as Marxism, tolerance (he wrote against liberalism and in favor of anarchism), political justification and democracy. Wolff is also well known for his work on Immanuel Kant.

Task 1　Generating the Outline

Directions: Please identify the thesis of the passage and the main point of each paragraph, and then find out how these points develop the thesis. You may use the table below for your help.

Para. 8: The thesis	The problem of "law or conscience" is very _____ . The line of demarcation where obedience ought to end and resistance must begin, is _____.
Para. 1: Socrates' opinion	A young person, if he stays in his country, must _____.
Para. 2: Socrates' opinion	A citizen should obey all of the laws all the time, _____.
Para. 3: Thoreau's opinion	If government sanctions acts, laws, or policies which are_____ _____, the citizen has no need to _____.
Para. 4: Thoreau's opinion	People cannot build a society of _____.
Para. 5: Wolff's opinion	A citizen has no duty to obey laws, even though he may _____ _____.
Para. 6: Author's analysis	The State is not an "intrinsic good" but an "instrumental good." The government assures order by _____ . So a morally sensitive individual would be required to _____.
Para. 7: Author's analysis	If the State becomes self-serving and tyrannical, the individual's obligation to _____ would _____.
Para. 8: Conclusion	We shouldn't obey to _____.

Task 2 Understanding the text

Directions: Please answer the following ten questions based on Text A.

1. According to Socrates what should a young person do if he stays in his country?
2. Why did Socrates think a citizen should obey the law?
3. Why did Thoreau say an individual must withdraw his support from government?
4. How do you understand the sentence "the true place for a just man is a prison"?
5. What is Thoreau's mode of resistance to government?
6. What did Wolff say about a moral agent?
7. What is "philosophical anarchism" according to Wolff?
8. How do you understand the sentence: a government is an "instrumental good"?
9. When does the author think the individual's obligation to obey the law should cease?
10. Why is the problem of "law or conscience" very complicated?

Task 3 Vocabulary Building

Directions: Compounding, joining two or more bases to form a new word, is a common device of word-formation in English. Such compound words can be nouns, adjectives or verbs. Now study the compound adjectives formed by n. + v.-ed in the box and complete the following sentences with them. Change the form where necessary.

| self-interested | sun-tanned | state-owned |
| heart-felt | school-based | snow-covered |

1. His strongly-built body and _____ skin make him look like a sportsman.
2. Her _____ body was found in Longwood Lane, Failand, by dog walkers on Christmas Day, eight days after she was reported missing.
3. It sounded tough-minded, and it offered Americans a simple and _____ reason for their young people to risk death in remote places.
4. The investigations have shifted from senior political figures to _____ companies and have also broadened out to the financial sector, including senior bank officials.
5. _____ health centers facilitate immunization services for adolescents with greater efficiency than community health centers.
6. If they refuse to make _____ apologies soon, we will have to bring an action against them.

Directions: Now study the following compound verbs formed by adv.+n. in the box and complete the sentences with them. Change the form where necessary.

| outlaw | underline | overload | off-load | outline | outrage |

1. They were _____ by the announcement of massive price increases.
2. The government will _____ the rebels unless they surrender immediately.
3. They should stop _____ waste from oil tankers into the sea.
4. This incident _____ the danger of travelling in the border area.
5. I think the President will _____ a vision for a more competitive America.
6. The lights fused because the system was _____ with electrical appliances.

Task 4 Learning the Phrases

Directions: Please fill in the blanks of the sentences below with the phrases listed in the box. Change the forms if necessary.

| acquaint oneself with | enter into | hint at | take note of | comply with |
| stop short of | reflect on | be guilty of | object to | at the expense of |

1. I may withhold the truth at times, but I _____ actually telling lies.
2. They will consider whether or not he has _____ serious professional misconduct.
3. The start of a new year is a good time to _____ the many achievements of the past.
4. Try to see and experience as much as you can, but before you jet off, _____ these tips.
5. A lot of people in the financial community are annoyed by these regulations because they are costly to _____ and they take a lot of resources.
6. It is an instrumental approach to _____ the culture of the target language in second language acquisition.
7. Conservatives _____ the cost, and the idea of what they say is just another bailout for the car industry.
8. The report is also believed to _____ the involvement of politicians, bureaucrats and mining lobbies.
9. Within developing countries, producers tend to gain from higher world prices _____ consumers.

10. The United States and Canada may _____ an agreement that would allow easier access to jobs across the border.

Task 5 Studying the Sentence Structure
Sentences with inverted word order
Sentences from the text
1. Should he stay, however, he must accept the duties of a citizen as the price of his rights. (Para. 1)
2. Should an individual object to a particular law, the contract requires him to obey it until he succeeds in securing a change through procedures for that purpose provided in the law. (Para. 2)
3. Not only did he eschew violence as a technique, but he readily accepted the penalty which the law provided for its violation to show that his motives were pure. (Para. 4)

Directions: Please follow the examples and create five inverted sentences on your own.
Tips:
1. In conditional clauses which talk about an unreal or impossible situation, if the conjunction word "if" is omitted, an inverted word order should be used.
2. In declarative sentences that begin with negative or restrictive words such as never, rarely, scarcely, hardly, ever, and not only, an inverted word order is often used.

1. _____
   _____.
2. _____
   _____.
3. _____
   _____.
4. _____
   _____.
5. _____
   _____.

Task 6 Paraphrasing Difficult Sentences
1. It would seem, then, for Socrates, that a citizen should obey all of the laws all the time, being neither selective nor inconsistent.
   _____
   _____.

2. Unless an individual wishes to be guilty of complicity in this morally despicable practice, he must withdraw his support from government now.
   _____
   _____.

3. Does the State have the authority to command obedience from the citizens, their own moral views notwithstanding?

4. If the State is not good in itself—an "intrinsic good," it is perhaps a necessary means to good—an "instrumental good."

5. As you do, you will probably find, as so many have, that "The speculative line of demarcation where obedience ought to end and resistance must begin, is faint, obscure, and not easily definable."

Task 7 Summarizing the Text

Directions: Please summarize Text A in about 150 words. You may use the table in Task 1 to help you.

Task 8 Writing with Comparison and Contrast

Directions: Study Paragraph 2 and Paragraph 3 carefully and write a passage of two paragraphs developed by comparison or contrast. Your writing should be about 200 words. You may choose one of the three topics in the box as your topic.

Tips:

1. The method of comparison and contrast is one of the dominant writing techniques in an expository essay. When a writer is comparing, he is pointing out the similarities that exist between objects, terms or ideas. When a writer is contrasting, though, he is focusing on the differences between objects, terms or ideas. In practice, however, comparison and contrast often appear together, because people generally compare two things that are similar in certain ways and different in others.

2. There are two major ways of organizing paragraphs of comparison and contrast. One way is to examine one thing thoroughly and then examine the other. The other way is to examine two things at the same time, discussing them point by point. If you are dealing with two rather broad topics, not too complex or detailed, you may use the first method. If your topics are complex or involve many small similarities or differences, it may be preferable to adopt the second way.

3. In text A the writer compared the different views of Socrates' and Thoreau's on whether a citizen should obey the law or not. In Paragraph 2, Socrates' opinions are presented, that is, a citizen should obey all of the laws all the time, being neither selective nor inconsistent. In Paragraph 3, Thoreau's ideas are given — a citizen should not be obedient to a law which he believes is immoral. So the first method is used to develop these two paragraphs.

> 1. the advantages of working in a large company and working in a small company
> 2. the disadvantages of online shopping and shopping in department stores
> 3. being a member of a group or the leader of a group

Part Three Reading and Speaking

Text B

Give Me Liberty or Give Me Death
Patrick Henry

1   No man thinks more highly than I do of the patriotism, as well as abilities, of the very worthy gentlemen who have just addressed the House. But different men often see the same subject *in different lights;* and, therefore, I hope it will not be thought disrespectful to those gentlemen if, entertaining as I do opinions of a character very opposite to theirs, I shall *speak forth* my *sentiments* freely and *without reserve*. This is no time for ceremony. The questing before the House is one of awful moment to this country. For my own part, I consider it as *nothing less than* a question of freedom or slavery; and *in proportion to* the *magnitude* of the subject ought to be the freedom of the debate. It is only in this way that we can hope to arrive at truth, and fulfill the great responsibility which we hold to God and our country. Should I keep back my opinions at such a time, through fear of giving offense, I should consider myself as guilty of *treason* towards my country, and of an act of disloyalty toward the Majesty of Heaven, which I *revere* above all *earthly* kings.

2   Mr. President, it is natural to man to *indulge in* the *illusions* of hope. We are apt to shut our eyes against a painful truth, and listen to the song of that *siren* till she transforms us into beasts. Is this the part of wise men, engaged in a great and *arduous* struggle for liberty? *Are* we *disposed to be* of the number of those who, having eyes, see not, and, having ears, hear not, the things which so nearly concern their *temporal salvation*? For my part, whatever *anguish* of spirit it may cost, I am willing to know the whole truth; to know the worst, and to *provide for* it.

3   I have but one lamp by which my feet are guided, and that is the lamp of experience. I know of no way of judging of the future but by the past. And judging by the past, I wish to know what there has been in the conduct of the British ministry for the last ten years to justify those hopes with which gentlemen have been pleased to *solace* themselves and the House. Is it that *insidious* smile with which our petition has been lately received? Trust it not, sir; it will prove a *snare* to your feet. Suffer not yourselves to be betrayed with a kiss. Ask yourselves how this gracious reception of our petition *comports* with those warlike preparations which cover our waters and darken our land. Are *fleets* and armies necessary to a work of love and reconciliation? Have we shown ourselves so unwilling to be reconciled that force must be called in to win back our love? Let us not *deceive* ourselves, sir. These are the *implements* of war and *subjugation*; the last arguments *to* which kings *resort*. I ask gentlemen, sir, what means

this *martial array*, if its purpose be not to force us to *submission*? Can gentlemen *assign* any other possible motive for it? Has Great Britain any enemy, in this quarter of the world, to call for all this *accumulation* of navies and armies? No, sir, she has none. They are meant for us: they can be meant for no other. They are sent over to bind and *rivet* upon us those chains which the British ministry have been so long *forging*. And what have we to oppose to them? Shall we try argument? Sir, we have been trying that for the last ten years. Have we anything new to offer upon the subject? Nothing. We have held the subject up in every light of which it is capable; but it has been all in vain. Shall we resort to *entreaty* and *humble supplication*? What terms shall we find which have not been already exhausted? Let us not, I *beseech* you, sir, deceive ourselves. Sir, we have done everything that could be done to *avert* the storm which is now coming on. We have petitioned; we have *remonstrated*; we have *supplicated*; we have *prostrated* ourselves before the *throne*, and have *implored* its interposition to arrest the tyrannical hands of the ministry and Parliament. Our petitions have been slighted; our *remonstrances* have produced additional violence and insult; our supplications have been *disregarded*; and we have been *spurned*, with *contempt*, from the foot of the throne! In vain, after these things, may we indulge the *fond* hope of peace and reconciliation. There is no longer any room for hope. If we wish to be free—if we mean to preserve those *inviolate* and *inestimable* privileges for which we have been so long *contending*—if we mean not *basely* to abandon the noble struggle in which we have been so long engaged, and which we have *pledged* ourselves never to abandon until the glorious object of our contest shall be obtained—we must fight! I repeat it, sir, we must fight! An appeal to arms and to the God of hosts is all that is left us!

4   They tell us, sir, that we are weak; unable to cope with so *formidable* an *adversary*. But when shall we be stronger? Will it be the next week, or the next year? Will it be when we are totally disarmed, and when a British guard shall be stationed in every house? Shall we gather strength by *irresolution* and inaction? Shall we acquire the means of *effectual* resistance by lying *supinely* on our backs and hugging the *delusive phantom* of hope, until our enemies shall have bound us hand and foot? Sir, we are not weak if we make a proper use of those means which the God of nature hath placed in our power. The millions of people, armed in the holy cause of liberty, and in such a country as that which we possess, are *invincible* by any force which our enemy can send against us. Besides, sir, we shall not fight our battles alone. There is a just God who *presides* over the *destinies* of nations, and who will raise up friends to fight our battles for us. The battle, sir, is not to the strong alone; it is to the *vigilant*, the active, the brave. Besides, sir, we have no election. If we were *base* enough to desire it, it is now too late to retire from the contest. There is no *retreat* but in submission and slavery! Our chains are forged! Their *clanking* may be heard on the plains of Boston! The war is inevitable—and let it come! I repeat it, sir, let it come.

5   It is in vain, sir, to *extenuate* the matter. Gentlemen may cry, Peace, Peace—but

there is no peace. The war is actually begun! The next *gale* that sweeps from the north will bring to our ears the clash of resounding arms! Our *brethren* are already in the field! Why stand we here idle? What is it that gentlemen wish? What would they have? Is life so dear, or peace so sweet, as to be purchased at the price of chains and slavery? Forbid it, Almighty God! I know not what course others may take; but as for me, give me liberty or give me death!

New Words

sentiment	[ˈsɛntəmənt]	n.	tender, romantic, or nostalgic feeling or emotion 情感,多愁善感
magnitude	[ˈmægnɪtuːd]	n.	greatness of size or amount; great importance or consequence 大小;重要性;(地震)级数
treason	[ˈtriːzn]	n.	a crime that undermines the offender's government 叛国,通敌
revere	[rɪˈvɪr]	v.	to respect and admire someone or something very much 尊敬,崇敬
earthly	[ˈɜːrθli]	a.	of or belonging to this earth as distinguished from heaven 地球的,世俗的
illusion	[ɪˈluːʒn]	n.	an idea or opinion that is wrong 幻想,幻觉
siren	[ˈsaɪrən]	n.	a piece of equipment that makes very loud warning sounds, used on police cars 汽笛,警报器
arduous	[ˈɑːrdʒuəs]	a.	difficult to accomplish; demanding considerable mental effort and skill 费力的,辛勤的
temporal	[ˈtɛmpərəl]	a.	relating to or limited by time; relating to practical instead of religious affairs 受时间限制的;尘世的
salvation	[sælˈveɪʃn]	n.	saving someone or sth. from harm of or from an unpleasant situation 拯救,救星
anguish	[ˈæŋgwɪʃ]	n.	extreme distress of body or mind 苦闷,痛苦
solace	[ˈsɑːləs]	v.	give moral or emotional strength to 安慰,慰藉
insidious	[ɪnˈsɪdiəs]	a.	happening gradually without being noticed and causing serious harm 潜伏的,阴险的
petition	[pəˈtɪʃn]	n.	a formal message requesting sth. that is submitted to an authority 请愿书,祈求
snare	[snɛr]	n.	sth. (often sth. deceptively attractive) that catches you unawares 陷阱,圈套
comport	[kəmˈpɔːrt]	v.	(with) behave well or properly (举止,行为)相称
fleet	[fliːt]	n.	group of aircraft, motor vehicles, steamships operating together under the same ownership 舰队,机群

deceive	[dɪˈsiːv]	v.	cause someone to believe an untruth 欺骗
implement	[ˈɪmplɪmənt]	n.	tool or instrument 工具，当工具用的物品
subjugation	[ˌsʌbdʒuˈgeɪʃn]	n.	the act of conquering 征服，镇压
martial	[ˈmɑːrʃl]	a.	related to the military and war 军队的，战争的
array	[əˈreɪ]	n.	an orderly arrangement 一系列，大批，队列
submission	[səbˈmɪʃn]	n.	being completely controlled by a person or group, and accepting that you have to obey them 屈从，屈服
assign	[əˈsaɪn]	v.	give a task to a person; select sth. or sb. for a specific purpose 布置（任务）；确定
accumulation	[əˌkjuːmjəˈleɪʃn]	n.	an increase by natural growth or addition 积累，积聚
rivet	[ˈrɪvɪt]	v.	to fasten with rivets（铆钉）铆接，固定
forge	[fɔːrdʒ]	v.	form by heating and hammering 锻造
entreaty	[ɪnˈtriːti]	n.	earnest or urgent request 恳求，哀求
humble	[ˈhʌmbl]	a.	low or inferior in station or quality 谦逊的，卑下的
supplication	[ˌsʌplɪˈkeɪʃn]	n.	a humble request for help from someone in authority 恳求，哀求
beseech	[bɪˈsiːtʃ]	v.	ask for or request earnestly 恳求，哀求
avert	[əˈvɜːrt]	v.	prevent from happening 避开
remonstrate	[rɪˈmɑːnstreɪt]	v.	argue in protest or opposition 抗议
supplicate	[ˈsʌplɪˌkeɪt]	v.	ask humbly (for sth.) 恳求，乞求
prostrate	[ˈprɑːstreɪt]	v.	stretched out and lying at full length along the ground 拜倒，倒下
throne	[θroʊn]	n.	the position and power of being a king or queen 王位，王权
implore	[ɪmˈplɔːr]	v.	ask for sth. in an emotional way 恳求，乞求
remonstrance	[rɪˈmɑːnstrəns]	n.	a complaint or protest 抱怨，抗议
disregard	[ˌdɪsrɪˈgɑːrd]	v.	treat as unimportant or unworthy of notice 忽视，不顾
spurn	[spɜːrn]	v.	refuse to accept showing no respect 轻蔑地拒绝
contempt	[kənˈtempt]	n.	(with ~) showing no respect 轻蔑
fond	[fɑːnd]	a.	foolish or silly 愚蠢的
inviolate	[ɪnˈvaɪələt]	a.	free from damage, injury or attack 未受打击的，未受损害的
inestimable	[ɪnˈestɪməbl]	a.	beyond calculation or measure 无价的，难以估量的
contend	[kənˈtend]	v.	compete against someone in order to gain sth. 竞争，争斗
basely	[ˈbeɪsli]	ad.	(old fashioned) in a despicable, ignoble manner 下贱地，卑鄙地
pledge	[pledʒ]	v.	promise solemnly and formally 保证，誓言
formidable	[ˈfɔːmɪdəbl]	a.	extremely impressive in strength or excellence 强大的
adversary	[ˈædvəseri]	n.	someone who offers opposition 敌手

Unit 5

irresolution	[ˌiˌrezəˈljuːʃən]	n.	doubt concerning two or more possible alternatives or courses of action 优柔寡断, 无决断
effectual	[iˈfektʃuəl]	a.	producing or capable of producing an intended result or having a striking effect 有效果的
supinely	[sʊˈpaɪnli]	ad.	with the face upward 仰卧地
delusive	[diˈluːsiv]	a.	inappropriate to reality or facts 迷惑人的, 虚假的
phantom	[ˈfæntəm]	n.	sth. existing in perception only 幻影, 幽灵
invincible	[inˈvinsəbl]	a.	incapable of being overcome or subdued 不可战胜的
preside	[priˈzaid]	v.	act as president 主持, 统辖
destiny	[ˈdestini]	n.	fate 命运
vigilant	[ˈvidʒilənt]	a.	being on the lookout for possible danger 警惕的
base	[beis]	a.	showing a lack of honor or morality 卑鄙的, 不道德的
retreat	[riˈtriːt]	n.	moving back; a place into which one can go for peace and safety 撤退; 隐居处
clank	[klæŋk]	v.	make a loud resonant repeating noise 发出叮当声
extenuate	[ikˈstenjueit]	v.	lessen the seriousness or extent of 减轻
gale	[geil]	n.	a strong wind 大风
brethren	[ˈbreðrən]	n.	(old fashioned) brothers 兄弟, 同胞

Phrases & Expressions

in a different / new light	from a different or new angle 从不同的/新的角度
speak forth	speak out 说出
without reserve	without restraint; frankly; freely 毫无保留
nothing less than	absolutely; completely 完全是; 无异于
in proportion to	agreeing in amount, magnitude, or degree 与……成比例
indulge in	let yourself do or have sth. that you enjoy, especially sth. bad for you 沉溺于, 纵情于
be disposed to do	feel willing to do sth. or behave in a certain way 有意于……
provide for	make plans in order to deal with sth. that might happen in the future 为……做准备
resort to	use sth. or do sth. bad in order to succeed or deal with a problem 诉诸, 求助于

1. "Give me liberty, or give me death!" is a quotation attributed to Patrick Henry from a speech he made to the Virginia Convention in 1775, at St. John's Church in Richmond, Virginia. He is credited with having swung the balance in convincing the Virginia House of Burgesses to pass a resolution delivering the Virginia troops to the Revolutionary War. Among the delegates to the convention were future U.S. Presidents Thomas Jefferson and George Washington.

2. Patrick Henry (1736—1799) was an American attorney, planter and politician who became known as an orator during the movement for independence in Virginia in the 1770s. A Founding Father, he served as the first and sixth post-colonial Governor of Virginia, from 1776 to 1779 and from 1784 to 1786. Henry led the opposition to the Stamp Act 1765 and is remembered for his "Give me liberty, or give me death!" speech. Along with Samuel Adams and Thomas Paine, he is regarded as one of the most influential champions of Republicanism and the American Revolution and its fight for independence. After the Revolution, Henry was a leader of the anti-federalists in Virginia. He opposed the United States Constitution, fearing that it endangered the rights of the States as well as the freedoms of individuals; he helped gain adoption of the Bill of Rights. By 1798 however, he supported President John Adams and the Federalists; he denounced passage of the Kentucky and Virginia Resolutions as he feared the social unrest and widespread executions that had followed the increasing radicalism of the French Revolution.

Task 1 Summarizing

Directions: Fill in the blanks in the following text outline with key points based on an overall understanding and then make an oral summary.

1. I shall speak forth my viewpoints freely and without reserve, for we are facing the critical moment of freedom or slavery.
2. We should not indulge in the illusions of _____.
3. British navies and armies are sent over to _____ which the British ministry have been so long forging. If we want to preserve _____, we have to _____.
4. We are not _____. Victory belongs to _____ because we have _____.
5. The war has actually begun. As for me, give me _____ or give me _____.

Task 2 Reflecting on the Text

Directions: You have just read Patrick Henry's speech "Give Me Liberty or Give Me Death." Discuss the passage with your partner and then give an oral presentation of your reflection on this speech.

Guiding Questions:
1. What are the most valuable things in your life?
2. Why are these things so precious to you?

Unit 5

3. Are you willing to sacrifice your life for your freedom? Why or why not?

Task 3 Making a Presentation

Directions: Give an oral presentation of your views on one of the following topics. You should state your views clearly.

1. Translate the following Chinese poem into English and make your comments on it.

   生命诚可贵，爱情价更高，若为自由故，两者皆可抛。

2. Make your comments on the statement: Government is the primary protector of an individual's rights and liberty.

Below are some expressions that you might find useful in your presentation.

> 1) Hungarian poet Petőfi Sándor
> 2) His responsibility is more important than his personal love affair.
> 3) defend and expand our rights and liberties
> 4) primary protector
> 5) violate people's basic rights and civil liberties
> 6) legislatures and courts
> 7) undermine our basic rights and freedoms
> 8) democratic government also functions as the main protector of our rights and freedoms
> 9) protect and enforce our individual rights
> 10) We rely on an active government to establish and maintain those rights.

Part Four Cross Cultural Communication

Passage A

贤能政府
林语堂

　　以一个国家为标准，吾们的政治生命中最显著的特点，为缺乏宪法，并缺乏公民权利之观念，这样的特点之存在，只因为一种特殊的社会和政治哲理、道德融合的哲理而不是一种效力的哲理。它把道德和政治混合在一起，成为一种宪法的基本概念，是在预断地把统治者当作坏坯子看待；他或许会滥用权力而损害我们的权力，吾们乃借重宪法为捍卫吾人权利的武器。中国对于政府的概念，恰与此预断直接地相反。中国人只知道政府是人民的父母，谓之"父母政府"，或者是"贤能政府"。他们将照顾人民之权利，一如父母之照料其子女，是以吾们人民把"便宜行事"的权利交托了政府，便予以无限的信任。在此等人手中，吾人托付数千百万的资产，从不一问其开支报告；吾们又赋予此辈以无限政治权力，亦从不计及自卫吾人之权益。吾们只把他们当作圣贤君子看待。

　　对此所谓贤能政府所下的批评，其精审、公平、正确，应无过于两千一百年以前韩非子的伟论，韩非子为属于法家之大哲学家，约生于孔子后三世纪。他是法家哲学派中最后亦为最伟大的一位，他的中心主张便是建立法制政府以代人治政府。他的分析人治政府之罪行极为精确，而他所描述的当时之政治生活现象极相类似于今日的中国，倘令韩非子复生而亲向吾人口述，亦将不易一字。

依照韩非子的意见，政治智慧之起点，始终摈弃道德之俗论并避免道德之改进。著者亦深信吾人停止谈论人民道德的感化愈早则吾人之能建立中国之廉洁政府亦将较早。可是事实上有那么许多人在议论着道德的改进，以为政治罪恶的解决手段，适足以说明他们思想之幼稚，和他们的领悟正确的政治问题之低能。他们应该明瞭吾人已经继续不断地谈道德的腐论历二千年之久，卒未能用道德之力量改进国家，或使她有一个比较贤明廉洁的政府。中国人民应该明瞭，倘令道德感化真能有何裨益，中国今日早已成为天使圣哲的乐园了。依著者愚见，用道德来改善政治的思想和议论，何以如是流行，特殊那些官吏们谈得尤为起劲，就因为他们知道这样的改革，至少不会有害于人。

韩非子时代有两种相对的政治概念，吾人在此现时代亦然。即孔子的贤能政府之概念和法治政府之概念，把每个统治者当作贤人君子，因而亦以对待贤人君子之礼遇之。法治制度的政治概念，则把每个统治者当作坏蛋看待，因进而制备种种条款，以防止其遂行歪曲意念。很清楚，前者是中国传统的见地，而后者是西洋的见地，亦即韩非子的见地。似韩非子所说："圣人之治国，不恃人之为吾善也，而用其不得为非也"，这就是法家哲学的道德观之基点。换言之，吾人不以统治者为君子而冀其行仁义之道，吾人应目之为潜伏的囚犯而筹谋种种方法与手段以期阻止此等可能的罪行，如剥削人民的权利与卖国。你可以很容易看出后者的制度是较易于收实效，其阻止政治腐化的效用，比之静待此等君子之良心发现高明得多。

 Notes

1. 本篇节选改编自林语堂的专著《吾国吾民》，191—193页。
2. 作者林语堂（1895—1976），福建龙溪人，是中国现代著名作家、学者、翻译家、语言学家，新道家代表人。原名和乐，后改玉堂，又改语堂。早年留学美国、德国，获哈佛大学文学硕士，莱比锡大学语言学博士。回国后在清华大学、北京大学、厦门大学任教。曾任联合国教科文组织美术与文学主任、国际笔会副会长等职。林语堂于1940年和1950年先后两度获得诺贝尔文学奖提名。曾创办《论语》《人世间》《宇宙风》等刊物，作品包括小说《京华烟云》《啼笑皆非》。散文和杂文文集《人生的盛宴》《生活的艺术》以及译著《东坡诗文选》《浮生六记》等。1966年定居台湾。1976年在香港逝世，享年80岁。

Word Bank

宪法	constitution	圣贤君子	gentlemen
政治哲理	political philosophy	韩非子	Hanfeitse
预断	presuppose	法家	legalist school
滥用权力	abuse their power	孔子	Confucius
父母政府	parental government	法制政府	government by law
道德感化	moralizations	歪曲意念	crooked intentions
赋予	give	廉洁政府	clean government
人治政府	government by persons	贤能政府	government by gentlemen
政治腐化	political corruption	行仁义之道	walk in the path of righteousness

Directions: Please summarize the passage in English. Your summary should be about 150—200 words.

Passage B

Resistance to Civil Government

Henry David Thoreau

  I heartily accept the motto, —"That government is best which governs least;" and I should like to see it acted up to more rapidly and systematically. Carried out, it finally amounts to this, which also I believe, —"That government is best which governs not at all;" and when men are prepared for it, that will be the kind of government which they will have. Government is at best but an expedient: but most governments are usually, and some governments are sometimes, inexpedient. The objectives which have been brought against a standing army, and they are many and weighty, and deserve to prevail, may also at last be brought against a standing government. The standing army is only an arm of the standing government. The government itself, which is only the mode which the people have chosen to execute their will, is equally liable to be abused and perverted before the people can act through it...

  But, to speak practically and as a citizen, unlike those who call themselves no-government men, I ask for, not at once no government, but at once a better government. Let every man make known what kind of government would command his respect, and that will be one step toward obtaining it.

  After all, the practical reason why, when the power is once in the hands of the people, a majority are permitted, and for a long period continue, to rule, is not because they are most likely to be in the right, nor because this seems fairest to the minority, but because they are physically the strongest. But a government in which the majority rule in all cases cannot be based on justice, even as far as men understand it.

  Can there not be a government in which majorities do not virtually decide right and wrong, but conscience? —In which majorities decide only those questions to which the rule of expediency is applicable? Must the citizen ever for a moment, or in the least degree, resign his conscience to the legislator? Why has every man a conscience, then? I think that we should be men first, and subjects afterward. It is not desirable to cultivate a respect for the law, so much as for the right. The only obligation which I have a right to assume, is to do at any time what I think right. It is truly enough said, that a corporation has no conscience; but a corporation of conscientious men is a corporation with a conscience...

  Thus the State never intentionally confronts a man's sense, intellectual or moral, but only his body, his senses. It is not armed with superior wit or honesty, but with superior physical strength. I was not born to be forced. I will breathe after my own fashion. Let us see who is the strongest...

  I do not wish to quarrel with any man or nation. I do not wish to split hairs, to make fine distinctions, or set myself up as better than my neighbors. I seek rather, I may say, ever an excuse for conforming to the laws of the land. I am but too ready to conform to them. Indeed I have reason to suspect myself on this head; and each year, as the tax-gatherer comes round, I find myself disposed to review the acts and position of the general and state governments, and the spirit of the people, to discover a pretext for conformity. I believe that the State will soon be able to take all my work of this sort out of my hands, and then I shall be no better a patriot than my fellow-countrymen. Seen from a lower point of view, the Constitution, with all its faults, is very good; the law and the courts are very respectable; even this State and this American government are, in many respects, very admirable and rare things, to be thankful for, such as a great many have described them; but seen from a point of view a little higher, they are what I have described them; seen from a higher still and the highest, who shall say what they are, or that they are worth looking at or thinking of at all?

The authority of government, even such as I am willing to submit to, —for I will cheerfully obey those who know and can do better than I, and in many things even those who neither know nor can do so well, —is still impure one: to be strictly just, it must have the sanction and consent of the governed. It can have no pure right over my person and property but what I concede to it. The progress from an absolute to a limited monarchy, from a limited monarchy to a democracy, is a progress toward a true respect for the individual. Is a democracy, such as we know it, the last improvement possible in government? Is it not possible to take a step further towards recognizing and organizing the rights of man? There will never be a really free and enlightened State, until the State comes to recognize the individual as a higher and independent power, from which all its own power and authority are derived, and treats him accordingly. I please myself with imagining a State at last which can afford to be just to all men, and to treat the individual with respect as a neighbor; which even would not think it inconsistent with its own repose, if a few were to live aloof from it, not meddling with it, nor embraced by it, who fulfilled all the duties of neighbors and fellow-men. A State which bore this kind of fruit, and suffered it to drop off as fast as it ripened, would prepare the way for a still more perfect and glorious State, which also I have imagined, but not yet anywhere seen.

1. The passage was retrieved and adapted from *Read a Bit of Philosophy* (Page 274—285).
2. It was originally written by Henry David Thoreau (1817—1862), who was an American author, poet, philosopher, abolitionist, naturalist, tax resister, development critic, surveyor and historian. A leading transcendentalist, Thoreau is best known for his book *Walden*, a reflection upon simple living in natural surroundings, and his essay *Resistance to Civil Government* (also known as *Civil Disobedience*), from which this passage is taken.

Word Bank

motto	名言	expedient	权宜之计
pervert	破坏	conscience	良心
applicable	可应用的	resign	屈从
legislator	立法者	subjects	臣民
assume	承担	corporation	团体
conscientious	有良心的	split hairs	吹毛求疵
distinction	卓越	conform	遵守
pretext	借口	conformity	遵从

sanction	授权	consent	准许
concede	让步	monarchy	君主制度
repose	宁静	aloof	避开
meddle	发生关系	embrace	包容
ripen	成熟		

Directions: Please summarize the passage in Chinese. Your summary should be about 200—300 words.

Unit 6

ECONOMY AND SOCIETY

"Things are disappearing right before our eyes," Belk writes. Our music "has come to reside somewhere inside our digital storage devices or on servers whose location we will never know." In other words, digital natives are growing up in a world where many of their possessions aren't actually physically possessed.

—From The "Dematerialization" of Society in the Digital Age

Learning Objectives

Upon the completion of this unit, you should be able to

Remembering & Understanding	★ read Text A and Text B aloud smoothly with expression indicative of comprehension and tone; ★ identify and explain in your own words the thesis and the major points of Text A and Text B;
Analyzing & Applying	★ use word building to compound a new word; ★ make reference to the thesis and/or the major points of Text A and Text B in your writing; ★ use sentences with adversative conjunctions for rhetoric effect;
Evaluating & Creating	★ incorporate writing skill "comparison & contrast" in developing paragraphs; ★ use information framework to retell the story; ★ deliver a clear and coherent oral presentation of your views on the impact of online shopping on society.

Unit 6

Part One Lead-in

Section 1 Listening: The Ice Bucket Challenge

Task 1 Filling the Blanks

Directions: Please fill in the blanks with one or two words on the basis of what you have heard.

If you logged on to Facebook over the weekend, chances are your newsfeed was flooded with videos of US celebrities drenching themselves in ice water. It seems everyone is getting in on the fun, from popular singers like Taylor Swift and Justin Timberlake, to _____ of tech including Bill Gates and Mark Zuckerberg.

Is it some kind of new, cool way to _____ the summer heat? Of course not.

It's a fundraising game called the Ice Bucket Challenge, and it aims to raise _____ for amyotrophic lateral sclerosis (ALS).

The challenge's _____ is straightforward. It involves daring a person to dump a bucket of ice water over their head within 24 hours, or _____ money toward fighting ALS. Even if a person completes the challenge, they're more than welcome to donate money anyhow.

Once a person completes the _____, they're supposed to issue the same challenge to several other people, usually three, which is why the challenge has been growing and growing.

Since the beginning of June, the game has spread across social media _____ and late-night talk shows in the US. According to Facebook, more than 15 million people so far have posted, commented, or liked a post about the challenge. It has raised more than $2.3 million (14 million yuan) to support research for the illness.

As for the origins of the craze, new data from the Facebook data science team heavily supports one theory: that the ice bucket challenge originated with Pete Frates, a former captain of the Boston College baseball team. Frates, 29, who was _____ ALS in 2012, can no longer speak and uses a wheelchair. After Frates posted his own ice bucket challenge video on July 31, the game took off and has now become one of the biggest stunts in the online _____.

Task 2 Group Discussion

Directions: Please discuss the following questions in pairs or groups based on what you have heard.

1. What is the origin of the game called the Ice Bucket Challenge?
2. What is the purpose of the game?
3. What is your attitude towards the game?

Section 2 Watching: Should You Donate Differently?

Task 1 Group Discussion

Directions: Please watch the video clip excerpted from "Should you donate differently?" and discuss the three questions below in pairs or groups.

1. Why did the author think unconditional cash transfer wasn't an effective way to help poor people 10 years ago?

2. What are the steps of the project called GiveDirectly?

3. Do you agree with the speaker? Why or why not?

Task 2 Summarizing the Text

Directions: Please summarize the passage in English. Your summary should be about 80—100 words.

Part Two Reading and Writing

Text A

The "Dematerialization" of Society in the Digital Age
Lee Peterson

1   A quarter century ago, Russell Belk introduced the concept of the extended self in a paper published in *the Journal of Consumer Research* and cited thousands of times since. The term was an *attempt* at explaining why "knowingly or unknowingly, intentionally or unintentionally, we regard our possessions as part of ourselves."

2   Possessions were one of the many ways we constructed an extended self, Belk argued. Of course, it wasn't exactly a new idea. In positing the *concept*, he *referenced* many academic and literary sources, including William James, who once wrote: "A man's self is the sum total of all that he can call his."

3   It was 1988. Teenage girls were *flocking* to local malls buying audio cassettes by the millions, catapulting George Michael's first solo album "Faith" to the top of the charts. As it had been for decades, many a first purchase—with real money—was being made inside the now defunct music stores Sam Goody and Camelot.

4   For decades, this common *rite of passage* into the adult world of commerce required the actual physical possession of the *commodity*. The object of desire sheathed in a protective layer of plastic needed unwrapping. There was the matter of storing and organizing one's good taste in orderly rows for others to see. A single technological stage earlier, teenagers were holding lustrous vinyl（黑胶唱片）instead.

5   Today, this formative act of *consumption* no longer requires we physically possess an object. Music, along with photos, videos, even our written words are "largely invisible and immaterial until we choose to *call* them *forth*," Belk, now a professor of marketing at York University, writes in an *update* to his ideas on the extended self in *Extended Self in a Digital World*, published this May.

6   Our digital age has *ushered in* five changes to the extended self, most interesting among them "dematerialization."

7   "Things are disappearing right before our eyes," Belk writes. Our music "has

come to reside somewhere inside our digital storage devices or on servers whose location we will never know." In other words, digital natives are growing up in a world where many of their possessions aren't actually physically possessed.

8   I mention Belk's take on "dematerialization" because it relates to a curious finding about how young people view ownership and the act of consumption in general. In a radical departure from *previous* generations, young people did not rank "instant ownership" as the most appealing feature of shopping, even though Boomers and Gen-X consumers did by an overwhelming margin, according to a recent quantitative survey of 1,700 consumers. Instead, young people ranked the "unlimited options" that online shopping *affords* as the most *appealing* aspect of buying. This research seems to suggest the instant gratification of "instant ownership" isn't what young people value most today — a shift that *shapes* how, why, and where they prefer to buy things.

9   And no wonder, it's not the kind of world they grew up in. No matter what the geographic or cultural limitations *inherited*, almost anything they want can be found and bought online, when and where they want it. This shift has potentially dramatic *implications* for the role of the physical store. After all, older generations grew up in a marketplace where options were *curtailed*, limited by the cultural and commercial milieu they inherited, restricted to the offerings at the local mall or Main Street commercial district. There was urgency to getting something now. The emotional reward of physically possessing something carried great *resonance*. It was the easiest way to contrast an extended self.

10   Young people today are more likely to mediate identity through the *perpetual* feedback loop of social media and online personae, though. At the moment of decision, this immediate feedback offers a way to mediate more than simply a purchase; one's sense of self within a community of peers is also *at stake*.

11   Perhaps this also explains why they ranked online consumer reviews as the second most appealing aspect of shopping, while Boomers and Gen-X shoppers ranked the tactile experience of "see and touch" as the second most appealing.

12   What does this mean for the future of our consumer culture? Can we still define so-called millennials as *materialistic*? This is a generation ushering in the "sharing economy," and transforming philanthropy with "crowdfunding（众筹）." Could this be the generation that radically alters the very meaning of ownership?

13   The findings seem to suggest a *fundamental* change in the way young people view material possessions and *approach* consumption. It's a shift with potentially massive implications for retailers. If the pleasures of "instant ownership" are waning and the *allure* of "unlimited options" *wins out,* are we about to enter a *permanent* era of retail rationalization?

14   Unbridled mall-based consumption—the kind that defined the Boomer and Gen-X generations—is unlikely to be as acceptable to twentysomethings. Some studies even suggest millennials might end up as frugal as their grandparents. Perhaps this

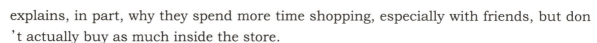

explains, in part, why they spend more time shopping, especially with friends, but don't actually buy as much inside the store.

15   Maybe knowing you can get something if you want it is more important than actually possessing it. Other research suggests this shift could benefit young people in the end, considering materialistic consumers *derive* more pleasure from desiring products than they do from actually owning them.

16   Previous generations, long *susceptible* to the allure of instant ownership, believed falsely possessing commodity objects could transform their identities.

17   Maybe young people just don't buy it anymore.

New Words

attempt	[əˈtem(p)t]	n.	an act of trying to do sth., esp. sth. difficult 努力，尝试，企图（尤指困难的事情）
concept	[ˈkɒnsept]	n.	an idea of how sth. is, or how sth. should be done 概念，观念，想法
reference	[ˈref(ə)r(ə)ns]	v.	written to mention another book, article etc. that contains information connected with the subject you are writing about 查阅，参考
flock	[flɒk]	v.	If people flock to a place, they go there in large numbers because sth. interesting or exciting is happening there 成群结队地去，蜂拥而至
commodity	[kəˈmɒdɪtɪ]	n.	a product that is brought and sold 商品
consumption	[kənˈsʌm(p)ʃ(ə)n]	n.	the act of buying and using products 购买，消费
update	[ʌpˈdeɪt]	n.	the most recent news or information about sth. 最新信息
digital	[ˈdɪdʒɪt(ə)l]	a.	using a system in which information is recorded or sent out electronically in the form of numbers, usually ones and zeros 数字的，数码的
previous	[ˈpriːvɪəs]	a.	having happened or existed before the event, time, or thing that you are talking about now 以前的，先前的
afford	[əˈfɔːd]	v.	to provide sth. or allow sth. to happen 提供，给予
appealing	[əˈpiːlɪŋ]	a.	attractive or interesting 有吸引力的，有趣的
shape	[ʃeɪp]	v.	to influence sth. such as a belief, opinion etc. and make it develop in a particular way 形成（某种信仰、看法等），影响（某事物的发展等）
inherit	[ɪnˈherɪt]	v.	to receive money, property etc. from someone after they have died 继承（遗产）
implication	[ˌɪmplɪˈkeɪʃən]	n.	a possible future effect or result of an action, event, decision etc. (行动、事件、决定等的)可能的影响或后果

Unit 6

curtail	[kɜːˈteɪl]	v.	to reduce or limit sth. 减少, 缩减, 削减, 限制
resonance	[ˈrez(ə)nəns]	n.	the special meaning or importance that sth. has for you because it relates to your own experiences (因与亲身经历有关而产生的) 共鸣
perpetual	[pəˈpetʃʊəl]	a.	continuing all the time without changing or stopping 连续不断的, 无休止的
materialistic	[məˌtɪərɪəˈlɪstɪk]	a.	concerned only with money and possessions rather than things of the mind such as art, religion, or moral beliefs 实利主义的, 物质主义的
fundamental	[fʌndəˈment(ə)l]	a.	relating to the most basic and important parts of sth. 根本的, 基本的, 基础的
approach	[əˈprəʊtʃ]	n.	a method of doing sth. or dealing with a problem 方法, 方式
allure	[əˈlʊə(r)]	n.	a mysterious, exciting, or desirable quality 诱惑, 魅力, 吸引力
permanent	[ˈpɜːm(ə)nənt]	a.	continuing to exist for a long time or for all the time in the future 长久的, 永久的, 永恒的
derive	[dɪˈraɪv]	v.	to get sth., esp. an advantage or pleasant feeling, from sth. 得到, 获得 (优势或愉快的感受)
susceptible	[səˈseptəbl]	a.	likely to suffer from a particular illness or be affected by a particular problem 易得病的, 易受影响的

Phrases & Expressions

rite of passage	a special ceremony or action that is sign of a new stage in someone's life (标志人生重要阶段的) 通过仪式
call forth	to produce a particular reaction 唤起, 引起, 激起
usher in	to cause sth. new to start, or to be at the start of sth. new 开创, 开始
at stake	if sth. that you value very much is at stake, you will lose it if a plan or action is not successful 有风险, 成败难料
win out	to finally succeed or defeat other people or things 终于成功

 **Notes**

1. The article by Lee Peterson was published in Salon, Aug. 27, 2013. Salon is a news website created by David Talbot in 1995 and part of Salon Media Group. It focuses on U.S. politics and current affairs, and on reviews and articles about music, books and films.
2. The author of the article, Lee Peterson, is executive vice president at WD Partners, a global design firm. His major works include: *How Can the Physical Store Satisfy the Next Generation of Shoppers (2013), Shopping Malls are Closing (2014), The Value of BOPIS (buy on line, pick up in store) (2014)*.
3. Generation X, commonly abbreviated to Gen X, is the generation born after the Western Post in World War II baby boom.
4. William James was an American philosopher and psychologist who was also trained as a physician.

Task 1 Generating the Outline

Directions: Please identify the thesis of the passage and the main point of each paragraph and find out how these points develop the thesis. You may use the table below to help you.

The thesis:	Young consumers _____.
Para. 1: Introduction	A quarter century ago, Russell Belk introduced the concept of _____ _____.
Para. 2: Introduction	_____ were one of the many ways we constructed an extended self.
Para. 3: The phenomenon	It was 1988 that teenage girls were flocking to local malls buying _____ _____.
Para. 4: The phenomenon	The rite of passage into the adult world of commerce required _____ _____.
Para. 5: The example	Today, _____ no longer requires we physically possess an object.
Para. 6: The explanation	The digital age has ushered in the most interesting of five changes to the extended self, that is, "_____."
Para. 7: The example	_____ are growing up in a world where many of their possessions aren't actually physically possessed.
Para. 8: The explanation	The instant gratification of "_____" isn't what young people value most today.
Para. 9: The explanation:	No matter what the geographic or cultural limitations inherited, almost anything young people today want _____.
Para. 10: The phenomenon	Young people today are more likely to mediate identity through _____ _____.

Unit 6

Para. 11: The consequence	Young people today ranked _____ as the second most appealing aspect of shopping.
Para. 12: The problem	This is a generation ushering in the _____.
Para. 13: The explanation	There is a fundamental change in the way _____.
Para. 14: The consequence	Millennials might end up _____.
Para. 15: The consequence	Knowing you can get something if you _____.
Para. 16: The phenomenon	Previous generations believed falsely _____.
Para. 17: The conclusion	Young people today _____ about instant ownership.

Task 2 Understanding the Text

Directions: Please answer the following ten questions based on Text A.

1. What is your understanding of the title "The 'Dematerialization' of Society in the Digital Age"?
2. What was the author's attitude towards "dematerialization", positive, neutral, or negative?
3. What is the purpose of putting forward the concept "extended self" by Russell Belk a quarter century ago? (Para. 1)
4. To go into the adult world of commerce, what should one do? (Para. 4)
5. What did the author mean when he wrote that "Our music has come to reside somewhere inside our digital storage devices or on servers whose location we will never know." (Para. 7)
6. What did Boomer and Gen-X consumers *by an overwhelming margin* rank as the most appealing feature of shopping? (Para. 8)
7. Why did the older generations have an urgency to get something now? (Para. 9)
8. Why did young people today rank online consumer reviews as the second most appealing aspect of shopping? (Para. 10)
9. Why did the studies suggest millennials might end up as frugal as their grandparents? (Para. 14)
10. What did previous generations believe falsely? (Para. 16)

Task 3 Vocabulary Building

Directions: Compounding is a word-formation process that joins two or more bases to form a new unit, a compound word. Now study compound nouns formed by n.+n. in the box and complete the following sentences with them. Change the form where necessary.

ownership	masterpiece	eyesight
aircraft	benchmark	mushroom

1. Jones said he wants to become a nuclear operator on an _____ carrier or a submarine.
2. The matter in dispute is the _____ of the house.
3. Every crystal was a _____ of design, and no one design was ever repeated.
4. This kind of _____ is edible, but that kind is not.
5. After one particular fall in 1919, she lost much of her _____.

6. We have rewritten all the sample scripts to cover the new _____.

Task 4　Learning the Phrases

Directions: Please fill in the blanks of the sentences below with the phrases listed in the box. Change the forms if necessary. Notice that some phrases need to be used more than once.

| call forth | usher in | at stake |
| regard as | derive from | susceptible to |

1. Globalization and the Internet, after all, were supposed to _____ an age in which people could live and work wherever they wanted
2. Nor does scientific knowledge _____ straightforwardly _____ experiments and observations.
3. Young people are most _____ advertisements.
4. _____ is not only the health of human beings but that of the earth.
5. Together, starting today, let us finish the work that needs to be done, and _____ a new birth of freedom on this Earth.
6. That's because those experiences are among your most important experiences in life, and your spouse should know anything you _____ important.
7. People don't just knock one another off like this unless there's big money _____.
8. The stereotype of German humourlessness is believed to _____ their reputation for efficiency, punctuality and rationality, presumed to be at the expense of humour.
9. When a race is in deepest stress and faced with great problems, it will _____ someone like Christ.
10. This is why Aristotle does not _____ the study of politics _____ one social science among others.
11. As long as we take adequate measures to _____ people's attention and their efforts, we can certainly prevent AIDS.
12. He is ambitious and _____ flattery.

Task 5　Studying the Sentence Structure

Sentences with adversative conjunctions

Sentences from the text

1. A single technological stage earlier, teenagers were holding lustrous vinyl *instead*. (Para. 4)
2. Young people today are more likely to mediate identity through the perpetual feedback loop of social media and online personae, *though*. (Para. 10)
3. Perhaps this also explains why they ranked online consumer reviews as the second most appealing aspect of shopping, *while* Boomers and Gen-X shoppers ranked the tactile experience of "see and touch" as the second most appealing. (Para. 11)
4. Perhaps this explains, in part, why they spend more time shopping, especially with friends, *but* don't actually buy as much inside the store. (Para. 14)

Unit 6

Directions: Please fill in the blanks of the sentences below with the adversative conjunctions listed in the box. Change the forms if necessary. Notice that some words or phrases need to be used more than once.

| but | though | only | on the contrary |
| however | yet | nevertheless | rather |

1. He did not succeed; _____, he failed long ago.
2. I don't know anything against that man; _____ I don't trust him
3. He is young. He is prudent, _____.
4. I am not idle. _____, I am very busy.
5. We respect him, _____ he has some faults.
6. The car was old, _____ it was in excellent condition.
7. She felt ill. She went to work, _____, and tried to concentrate.
8. He is a millionaire, _____ on the other hand a drunkard.

Task 6 Paraphrasing Difficult Sentences

1. This research seems to suggest the instant gratification of "instant ownership" isn't what young people value most today—a shift that shapes how, why, and where they prefer to buy things.

   _____
   _____.

2. After all, older generations grew up in a marketplace where options were curtailed, limited by the cultural and commercial milieu they inherited, restricted to the offerings at the local mall or Main Street commercial district.

   _____
   _____.

3. Young people today are more likely to mediate identity through the perpetual feedback loop of social media and online personae though.

   _____
   _____.

4. This is a generation ushering in the "sharing economy," and transforming philanthropy with "crowdfunding."

   _____
   _____.

5. Previous generations, long susceptible to the allure of instant ownership, believed falsely possessing commodity objects could transform their identities.

   _____
   _____.

Task 7 Summarizing the Text

Directions: Please summarize Text A in 100 words. You may use the table in Task 1 to help you.

Task 8　Writing with Comparison & Contrast

Directions: Write a passage of two paragraphs on "which one is better: online shopping or traditional shopping." In the first paragraph, you should summarize the author's view and state your own opinion. In the second paragraph, you should compare online shopping with traditional shopping to support your point. Your writing should be about 200 words. You may use what is provided in the box below to help you.

Tips:

1. The method of comparison and contrast is a good way to develop paragraphs. For instance, when talking about how young people view ownership and the act of consumption in general, the text says *"In a radical departure from previous generations, young people did not rank "instant ownership" as the most appealing feature of shopping, even though boomers and gen-X consumers did by an overwhelming margin."*

2. A comparison points out the similarities between two or more persons or things of the same class, while contrast, the differences between them. In practice, however, comparison and contrast often appear together, because people generally compare two things that are similar in certain ways and different in others. The following words and phrases are often used in making comparison and contrast.

To compare:

similar to, similarly, as, like, likewise, correspond to, resemble, almost the same as, at the same rate as, (just) as...as, in like manner, in the same way, have...in common, be parallel in, equally important, accordingly

To contrast:

unlike, while, whereas, however, still, nevertheless, otherwise, but, although, even so, not only...but also, the former...the latter, on the one hand...on the other, different from, in contrast to, in opposition to, on the contrary, on the other hand, on the opposite side, less/more/faster than, despite, in spite of, once...now

---

　　Lee Peterson, executive vice president and columnist, once expressed his view about online shopping. According to him, [...]. In my opinion, Lee Peterson's argument is well-justified.

　　Compared with traditional shopping, online shipping has a lot of advantages [...]

Part Three Reading and Speaking

Text B

Lost Generation: Pain of Privilege and Plight of the Poor
—Where's Society going Wrong
Terence Blacker

1   On one side of the Atlantic, an academic survey *reveals* the pain of privilege for the children of moneyed families. Here, a former Prime Minister, who once promised to deliver a genuinely classless society, has described the continuing—indeed, growing— power of the *affluent* and privately educated in this country as "truly shocking." Oddly, the findings of researchers at Arizona State University and the speech this week by John Major lead to a similar conclusion. To become a happier society, and one less wasteful of its citizens' talent, we need to become less divided by class. The sons and daughters of the relatively rich, to whom much is given and from whom much is expected, tend to *buckle* under the pressure. According to the American survey, published in *Psychology Today*, the children of families which earn the equivalent of £100,000 or more are twice as likely as their peers to suffer from anxiety, depression and mental illness leading to *addiction* and self-harm.

2   It is not just the usual pushy parents who are to blame, the report says. "Impossibly high expectations are *transmitted* by the entire community—teachers, schools, coaches and peers." Those at the other end of the social *scale*, whose problem is precisely the opposite, are hardly likely to be models of contentment either.

3   It is a depressing and morale-sapping message that is being handed down to the generation now reaching adulthood, with too much expectation on those from a certain background and not enough for many of the rest.

4   The education of the past, for all its faults, had at its core the idea that a person should do his or her best in life, that not everyone can be top. Today, children *deemed* to have ability find themselves under increasing pressure to pass exams as their education progresses. The anxious competitiveness of schools allows less and less time for learning as play and curiosity, for developing the whole person. Such is the importance of exams, that a child who has been predicted A grades in her exams is being set up for disappointment. When future success is assumed, there is only one way to go. It is the worst, most stressful kind of pressure?

5   Our fretful culture, in which achievement is only real if it is visible on a league table or a salary *slip* often fails to pass on the knack of happiness, of growing into your

own capabilities and strengths in your own time, without having to deal with impossible hopes or crushing *limitations*.

6 Never has that strong sense of self been more necessary for professional *survival*. The model of business success presented through the media is both ugly and unrealistic. It starts with a group of unpleasant young people on the *Apprentice* trying to do each other down and *curry favour* with the sour-faced business guru K Alan Sugar. It continues with people trying to *set up* their own businesses being *humiliated* on Dragons' Den. It ends, by a *miraculous* process that no one will be able to explain, in the annual wet dream: of financial triumph that is the Sunday Times Rich List.

7 Away from business, the middle-class profession—politics, the law, medicine—are seen increasingly as bastions of privilege, while the media is an ever-shrinking shark-pool.

8 There are, of course, endless *entertainment* possibilities in the strivings, and more often than not the failures, of those outside the circle of *advantage*. At the showbusiness end of the scale, the trick is to present success not as something which is the result of work, *application*, even passing exams, but as a *bolt* of good fortune, or a sudden flash of talent, which can *descend* on a lucky person as if they were in a film or story.

9 It might be competing on *The X Factor*. It could be the overnight stardom of a teenage footballer. Or a young cook discovered by a TV chef or a pretty face that *appeals to* a model agency. These dramatic changes of fortune play very well in schools where other, more conventional routes to achievement are *scarcely* considered.

10 Anyone who has visited a school in a relatively poor area will know that not only do the children dream of fame and instant public success, but their parents *play along with* the fantasy. After a children's book event at a literary festival, a sweet, slightly *plump* reader of about 11 told me that her ambition was one day to be an author or a lawyer. Her only problem was her parents; they were determined that she should be a model.

11 Meanwhile, the world of the unprivileged has become a regular staple of entertainment—sometimes a source of guilty humour—for those more fortunate. On any night the week, you will find a programme exploring, in the usual tone of concern, some horror story from the underclass. It might be obesity, or youth crime, or drunkenness, or teenage *pregnancy*. The trap of class remains, as John Major points out, but *all the same* those entering the job market become consumers. Television *commercials* by banks, insurance agencies, or larger retail outlets, have an increasingly childish vibe, and have taken to presenting a gentle, escapist view of the world, with dogs and balloons and smiling grannies.

12 In this year's Christmas commercials for Marks & Spencer and John Lewis, the products being sold remain unseen and even the idea of giving presents to others is only hinted at. We are in fairy-tale world of *Alice in Wonderland or Disney's fantasia*. Society may give more to the privileged, and professional life might be more brutally selfish

than ever, but the image of our society provided by big business is infantilized, a sort of paradise of perfect *generosity*.

13   Back in the 1990s, John Major *claimed* that his government would *herald* a new Britain that was confident and at ease with itself. Many of those born when that promise was made have grown up to be neither confident nor at ease with themselves, and that should be a source of shame.

New Words

reveal	[rɪˈviːl]	v.	to make known sth. that was previously secret or unknown 揭示, 揭露, 透露
affluent	[ˈæfluənt]	a.	having plenty of money, nice houses, expensive things etc. 富裕的, 富足的
buckle	[ˈbʌkl]	v.	to become bent or curved because of heat or pressure, or make sth. bend or curve in this way (因高温或压力)(使)弯曲, (使)扭曲, (使)变形
addiction	[əˈdɪkʃ(ə)n]	n.	the need to take a harmful drug regularly, without being able to stop 瘾
transmit	[trænzˈmɪt]	v.	to send or pass sth. from one person, place or thing to another 传递, 传播
scale	[skeɪl]	n.	a whole range of different types of people or things, from the lowest level to the highest 等级, 级别
deem	[diːm]	v.	to think of sth. in a particular way or as having a particular quality 认为, 视为
slip	[slɪp]	n.	a small or narrow piece of paper 小纸片, 纸条
limitation	[lɪmɪˈteɪʃ(ə)n]	n.	qualities that stop someone or sth. from being as good or as effective as you wish they could be (某人或某事物的)局限性, 不足之处
survival	[səˈvaɪv(ə)l]	n.	the state of continuing to live or exist 继续生存, 幸存
apprentice	[əˈprentɪs]	n.	someone who works for an employer for a fixed period of time in order to learn a particular skill or job 学徒, 徒弟
humiliate	[hjʊˈmɪlɪeɪt]	v.	to make someone feel ashamed or stupid, especially when other people are present 使羞辱, 蒙羞
miraculous	[mɪˈrækjʊləs]	a.	very good, completely unexpected, and often very lucky 不可思议的, 神奇的, 非凡的
entertainment	[entəˈteɪnm(ə)nt]	n.	things such as films, television, performances etc. that are intended to amuse or interest people 娱乐节目, 娱乐活动

advantage	[əd'vɑːntɪdʒ]	n.	sth. that helps you to be more successful than others, or the state of having this 有利条件，优势
application	[ˌæplɪ'keɪʃ(ə)n]	n.	attention or effort over a long period of time 专心，努力，勤奋
bolt	[bəʊlt]	n.	lighting that appears as a white line in the sky 闪电，雷劈
descend	[dɪ'send]	v.	if darkness, silence, a feeling etc descends, it becomes dark etc you start to feel sth., especially suddenly（黑暗、寂静等突然）降临；（感情等突然）袭来，来临
scarcely	['skeəslɪ]	ad.	almost not or almost none at all 几乎不，几乎没有
plump	[plʌmp]	a.	slightly at in a fairly pleasant way 丰满的，胖乎乎的
pregnancy	['pregnənsɪ]	n.	when a woman is pregnant (= has a baby growing inside her body) 怀孕（期），妊娠（期）
commercial	[kə'mɜːʃ(ə)l]	n.	an advertisement on television or radio （电视或电台的）商业广告
generosity	[dʒenə'rɒsətɪ]	n.	a generous attitude, or generous behaviour 慷慨，大方
claim	[kleɪm]	v.	to state that sth. is true, even though it has not been proved 声称，断言，主张
herald	['her(ə)ld]	v.	to be a sign of sth. that is going to come or happen soon 预示……的发生

Phrases & Expressions

curry favour (with)	to try to make someone like you or notice you in order to get sth. that you want 讨好，奉承，拍马屁
set up	to start a company, organization, committee etc 建立，成立，创立（公司、机构、委员会等）
appeal to	if someone or sth. appeals to you, they seem attractive and interesting 有吸引力
play along with	to pretend to agree to do what someone wants, in order to avoid annoying them or to get an advantage 假意顺从，暂且附和
all the same	in spite of this 虽是这样，尽管如此

Unit 6

 **Notes**

1. The article was published in *The Independent,* Nov.11, 1993. *The Independent* is a British national morning newspaper published in London by Independent Print Limited.
2. Terence Blacker is an English author, columnist, journalist, and publisher. He regularly writes as a columnist.
3. *The Sunday Times* is the largest-selling British national "quality" Sunday newspaper.
4. The X Factor is a television music competition franchise created by Simon Cowell.

Task 1 Summarizing

Directions: Fill in the blanks in the following text outline with key points based on an overall understanding and then make an oral summary.

I. To become a happier society, we _____
II. 1. The middle-class youth is easier to _____
    2. Reasons:
    a. Impossibly high expectations are _____
    b. The fault of the education today _____
    c. The model of business success presented _____
    d. A good fortune _____
    e. The unprivileged _____
    f. The image of our society provided by big businesses _____
III. John Major's promise

Task 2 Reflecting on the Text

Directions: You have just read the passage entitled "Lost generation: pain of privilege and plight of the poor — where's society going wrong?" Discuss the following questions with your partner and then give an oral presentation by linking up your answers to the questions.

Guiding Questions:
1. To become a happier society, what should we do?
2. What should be blamed for depressed middle-class youth?
3. What is the core idea of the education of the past? How about today?
4. What is the shortcoming of our fretful culture?
5. What is the trick at the showbusiness?
6. What does the author want to tell us through citing the example of this year's Christmas commercials for Marks & Spencer and John Lewis?
7. How do people in Britain today feel about John Major's promise?

Task 3 Making a Presentation

Directions: Give an oral presentation of your views on the topic "How to cope with stress." You should state your view clearly. Use the following outline as a help.

1. the definition of stress
2. the positive and negative effects of stress
3. the good ways of coping with negative effects of stress

Below are some words and expressions that you might find useful in your presentation.

1) tension	2) pressure
3) motivate	4) hinder
5) lead to	6) physical illness
7) metal health	8) meditation
9) aerobic exercise	10) social support

Part Four Cross Cultural Communication

Passage A

给自己一个梦想

马 云

作为一个创业者,首先要给自己一个梦想。1995年,我偶然有一次机会到了美国,然后我发现了互联网。所以回来以后我叫了24个朋友到我家里,大家坐在一起,我说我准备从大学里辞职,要做一个互联网。两个小时以后大家投票表决,23个人反对,一个人支持,大家觉得这个东西肯定不靠谱。别去做那个,你电脑也不懂,而且根本不存在这么个网络。但是经过一个晚上的思考,第二天早上我决定,我还是辞职,去做,去实现我自己的梦想。那为什么是这样呢?我发现,今天我回过头来想,我看见很多优秀的年轻人,是晚上想想千条路,早上起来走原路。晚上充满激情地说,明天我将干这个事,第二天早上仍然走自己原来的路线。如果你不去采取行动,不给自己梦想一个实践的机会,你永远没有机会,所以呢,我稀里糊涂地走上了创业之路,我把自己称作是一个盲人骑在一个瞎的老虎上面,所以根本不明白将来会怎么样。但是我坚信互联网将会对人类社会有很大的贡献。

有了一个理想之后,我觉得,最重要的是给自己一个承诺,承诺自己要把这件事情做出来,很多创业者都想想这个条件不够,那个条件没有,这个条件也不具备。该怎么办? 我觉得创业者最重要的是创造条件,如果机会都成熟的话,一定轮不到我们。所以呢,一般大家都觉得这是个好机会,一般大家都觉得机会成熟的时候,我认为往往不是你的机会,你坚信事情能够起来的时候给自己一个承诺说,我准备干5年,我准备干10年,干20年,把它干出来,我相信你就会走得很久。

另外一个呢,我想创业者一定要想清楚三个问题:第一,你想干什么? 不是你父母让你干什么,不是你同事让你干什么,也不是别人在干什么你需要干什么,而是你自己到底想干什么? 想清楚干什么的时候,你要想清楚我该干什么,而不是我能干什么。创业之前,很多人问,我有这个,我能干这个,所以我一定干得比别人好。我一直坚信,这个世界上比你能干,比你有条件干的人很多,但比你更想干好这个事情的人全世界应该只有你一个。这样你就有机会赢。

所以想清楚干什么,然后就要清楚该干什么,该干什么要明白自己不该干什么,在创业的过程中,四五年以内,我相信任何一家创业公司,都会面临很多的抉择和机会。在每个抉择和机会过程中,你是不是还是和第一天,像自己初恋那样,记住自己的第一天的梦想,至关紧要。在原则面前,你能不能坚持,在诱惑面前,你能不能坚持原则。在压力面前你能不能坚持原则,最后想干什么,该干什么以后,再跟自己说,我能干多久,我想干多久,这件事情该干多久就干多久。

所以呢,9年的经历告诉我,没有条件的时候创造条件,只要你有梦想,只要你有良好的团队,坚定的执行,你是能够走到大洋的那一岸。最后,我想跟所有的创业者和准备创业的共勉,还是我自己每天跟自己讲的那句话,今天很美好,明天更残酷,但后天很美好。绝大部分人死在明天晚上。所以我们必须每天努力面对今天。

 Notes

1. 马云是阿里巴巴集团、淘宝网、支付宝创始人。
2. 本篇是马云的一篇演讲稿,收录在由张燕撰写的《马云:我的世界永不言败》一书中。

Word Bank

互联网	internet	创业者	entrepreneur
辞职	resign	初恋	first love
采取行动	take action	原则	principle
承诺	promise	诱惑	temptation
成熟	mature	残酷	cruel

Directions: Please summarize the passage in English. Your summary should be about 150—200 words.

Passage B

Integrity

Warren Buffett

I would like to talk for just one minute to the students about your future when you leave here. Because you will learn a tremendous amount about investments, you all have got the ability to do well; you all have got the IQ to do well. You all have got the initiative and energy to do well or you wouldn't be here. Most of you will succeed in meeting your aspirations. But in determining whether you succeed there is more to it than intellect and energy. I would like to talk just a second about that. In fact, there was a fellow, Pete Kiewit in Omaha, who used to say, he looked for three things in hiring people: integrity, intelligence and energy. And he said that if the person did not have the first two, the later two would kill him, because if they don't have integrity, you want them dumb and lazy, you don't want them smart and energetic.

And I'd really like to talk about the first one because we know you have the last two. Play along with a little game for just a second in terms of thinking about that question. You have all been here, I guess almost of you are second-year MBAs, so you got to know your classmates for the rest of his or her lifetime. You can't pick one with a rich father, that doesn't count; you have got to pick somebody who is going to do it on his or her own merit. And I give you an hour to think about it, which one you're gonna pick among all your classmates, the one you wanna own 10 percent of for the rest of your lifetime.

Are you going to give them an IQ test and pick the one with the highest IQ? I doubt it. Are you going to pick the one with the best grades? I doubt it. You're not gonna pick the one who's the most energetic as well because you are the one who displays it in some issues. You are going to start looking for qualitative factors, in addition to the quantitative, because everyone has enough brains and energy. I would say that if you thought about it for an hour and decide who you're gonna place that bet on, you probably pick the one who you responded the best to, the one who are going to have the leadership qualities, the one who was going to get other people to carry out their interests. That would be the person who was generous, honest and who gave credit to other people even for their own ideas. All kinds of qualities like that. You can write down those qualities that you admire on such person, whoever you admire most in the class.

Then I would throw in a hooker. And I would say, as part of owning 10% of this person, you had to really go short 10% as somebody else in the class. This is more fun, isn't it? And you would think "who do I really wanna go short?" And again, you wouldn't pick the person with the lowest IQ, You would think about the person really who turned you off for one person or another. They had various qualities quite apart from their academic achievement. You didn't want to be around them, and other people didn't want to be around them. What are their qualities that lead to that? It could be a bunch of things but it is the person who is egotistical, and it is the person who is slightly dishonest, cuts corners, all of these qualities. And you can write those down on the right hand side of the page.

As you look at those qualities on the left and right hand side, there is one interesting thing about them: It is not the ability to throw a football 60 yards, it is not the ability to run the 100 yard dash in 9.3 seconds, it is not being the best looking person in the class—they are all qualities that if you really want to have the ones on the left hand side, you can have them. I mean their qualities, behavior, temperament, character that are achievable. They are not forbidden to anybody in this group. And if you look at qualities on the right hand side, the ones that you find turn you off in other people, there is not a quality there that you have to have. If you have it, you can get ride of it. And you get ride a lot easier your age than you can at my age because most behaviors are habitual and they say the chains of habit are too light to be felt until they are too heavy to be broken. There is no question about that.

I see people with these self-destructive behavior patterns at my age or even ten to twenty years younger and they really are entrapped by them. They go around and do things that turn off other people right and left. They don't need to be that way but by a certain point they get so they can hardly change it. But at your age you can have any habits, any patterns of behavior that you wish. It is simply a question of which you decide. And why not decide the ones that...I mean, if you like...

Ben Graham did this, Ben Franklin did this before him, but Ben Graham did this in his low teens. Ben Graham did this in his low teens and he looked around at the people he admired and he said, you know, "I want to be admired, so why don't I behave like them?" and he found there is nothing impossible about behaving like them. He did the same thing on the reverse side in terms of getting ride of those qualities.

So I would suggest that if you write those qualities down and think about them a little while and make them habitual, you will be the one that you want to buy 10% off when you get old and you already own 100% of yourself. You are stuck with it so you might as well be that person, that somebody else.

1. The passage is a lecture given by Warren Edward Buffet (1930—) at School of Business in University of Florida, 1998.
2. Warren Buffett is an American business magnate, investor and philanthropist.

Directions: Please summarize the passage in Chinese. Your summary should be about 200—300 words.

Unit 7

MAN AND NATURE

It may be said that natural selection is daily and hourly scrutinizing, throughout the world, every variation, even the slightest; rejecting that which is bad, preserving and adding up all that is good; silently and insensibly working, whenever and wherever opportunity offers, at the improvement of each organic being in relation to its organic and inorganic conditions of life.

—From *Natural Selection* by Charles Darwin

Learning Objectives

Upon the completion of this unit, you should be able to

Remembering & Understanding	★ read Text A and Text B aloud smoothly with expression indicative of comprehension and tone; ★ identify and explain in your own words the thesis and the major points of Text A and Text B;
Analyzing & Applying	★ make reference to the thesis and/or the major points of Text A and Text B in your writing; ★ understand sentences or clauses with *it-extraposition*;
Evaluating & Creating	★ develop cause and effect essays in expository writing; ★ make reflections about relationship between man and nature; ★ deliver a clear and coherent oral presentation of your views on the impact of human behavior on nature.

Unit 7

Part One Lead-in

Section 1 Listening: Plant Life

Task 1 Filling the Blanks

Directions: Please fill in the blanks with one or two words on the basis of what you have heard.

A: I'm Chrisopher Cruise.

B: And I'm Mario Ritter with EXPLORATIONS in VOA Special English. Today we tell about concerns about plant life, including agricultural crops. And we tell about efforts to keep them growing in the years to come.

A: Agricultural experts say crop _____ is important to feed the increasing population of our planet. They say having a large variety of plants also helps to protect against possible crop diseases and future _____. Hundreds of thousands of different plants now exist. But many experts say the number has decreased sharply during the past century. One of the world's largest seed projects has predicted further losses. The Millennium Seed Bank Partnership is warning that up to one hundred thousand plant species could permanently disappear. The rich _____ of genes that decide their qualities would disappear with them.

B: Many experts _____ climate change and loss of habitat, normal growth area, for damaging plant life. They say human activities and poorly planned, overly _____ of land are also responsible. The United Nations Food and Agriculture Organization says modern business farming is responsible for loss of farmers' traditional crop varieties. The "Green Revolution" of the twentieth century changed agriculture. Some experts say the use of modern _____ farming methods saved millions of people from _____. Farmers planted, watered, and fertilized their crops with the help of machines. They treated their fields with chemicals to control insects and diseases. Harvests grew larger and higher quality. But another result was that some traditional crops were lost.

A: The Food and Agriculture Organization says about two hundred fifty thousand plant species are now known to exist. The FAO notes that today, thirty thousand plant species could be eaten. Still, it says, only seven thousand have been used for food. About one hundred twenty crops are grown to feed humans. The FAO says nine of those crops _____ seventy five percent of human food. Rice, wheat and maize are said to _____ more than half of human food.

Task 2 Group Discussion

Directions: Please discuss the following questions in pairs or groups based on what you have heard.

1. According to the speakers, what should be responsible for damaging plant life?
2. Can you describe the current situation of human food supply?
3. Can you predict the future condition of plant life?

Section 2　Watching: Understanding the Natural World

Task 1　Group Discussion

Directions: Please watch the video "Understanding the Natural World" and discuss the following questions in pairs or groups.

1. What can be regarded as the fruits of people's endeavours in the 19th century?
2. How did Darwin explain the way different species evolved?
3. How do you explain that all life was inter-related?

Task 2　Summarizing

Directions: Please watch the video again, and try to summarize the main idea.

Part Two　Reading and Writing

Text A

Natural Selection
Charles Darwin

1　　Can the principle of selection, which we have seen is so *potent* in the hands of man, apply in nature? I think we shall see that it can act most effectually. Let it be *borne in mind* in what an endless number of strange *peculiarities* our domestic productions, and, in a lesser degree, those under nature, vary; and how strong the hereditary tendency is. Under domestication, it may be truly said that the whole organisation becomes in some degree plastic. Let it be borne in mind how infinitely complex and close-fitting are the mutual relations of all *organic* beings to each other and to their physical conditions of life. Can it, then, be thought improbable, seeing that *variations* useful to man have undoubtedly occurred, that other variations useful in some way to each being in the great and complex battle of life, should sometimes occur in the course of thousands of generations? If such do occur, can we doubt (remembering that many more individuals are born than can possibly survive) that *individuals having any advantage*, however slight, *over* others, would have the best chance of surviving and of procreating their kind? On the other hand, we may feel sure that any variation in the least degree injurious would be *rigidly* destroyed. This preservation of favorable variations and the rejection of injurious would not be affected by natural selection, and would be left a *fluctuating* element, as perhaps we in the species called polymorphic.

2　　We shall best understand the probable course of natural selection by taking the case of a country undergoing some physical change, for instance, of climate. The proportional numbers of its *inhabitants* would almost immediately undergo a change, and some species might become extinct. We may conclude, from what we have seen of the intimate and complex manner in which the inhabitants of each country are bound together, that any change in the numerical proportions of some of the inhabitants, independently of the change of climate itself, would most seriously affect many of the others. If the country were open on its borders, new forms would certainly *immigrate*, and this also would seriously disturb the relations of some of the former inhabitants. Let it be remembered how powerful the influence of a single introduced tree or *mammal* has been shown to be. But in the case of an island, or of a country partly surrounded by barriers, into which new and better adapted forms could not freely enter, we should then have places in the economy of nature which would assuredly *be* better *filled up*, if some of the original inhabitants were in some manner *modified*; for, had the area been open to immigration, these same places would have been seized on by *intruders*. In such cases, every slight modification, which *in the course of* ages chanced to *arise*, and which in any way favoured the individuals of any of the species, by better adapting them to their altered conditions, would tend to be preserved; and natural selection would thus have free *scope* for the work of improvement.

3   As man can produce and certainly has produced a great result by his *methodical* and unconscious means of selection, what may not nature effect? Man can act only external and visible characters: nature cares nothing for appearances, *except in so far as* they may be useful to any being. She can act on every internal organ, on every shade of *constitutional* difference, on the whole machinery of life. Man selects only for his own good; nature only for that of the being which she tends. Every selected character is fully exercised by her; and the being is placed under well-suited conditions of life. Man keeps the natives of many climates in the same country; he seldom exercises each selected character in some peculiar and fitting manner; he feeds a long and a short beaked pigeon on the same food; he does not exercise a long-backed or long-legged quadruped（四足动物）in any peculiar manner; he exposes sheep with long and short wool to the same climate. He does not allow the most *vigorous* males to struggle for the females. He does not rigidly destroy all inferior animals, but protects during each varying season, as far as lies in his power, all his productions. He often begins his selection by some half-monstrous form; or at least by some modification *prominent* enough to *catch his eye*, or to be plainly useful to him. Under nature, the slightest difference of structure or constitution may well turn the nicely-balanced scale in the struggle for life, and so be preserved. How fleeting are the wishes and the efforts of man! How short his time and *consequently* how poor will his products be, compared with those accumulated by nature during whole geological periods. Can we wonder, then, that nature's productions should be far "truer" in character than man's productions; that they should be infinitely better adapted to the most complex conditions of life, and should plainly bear the stamp of far higher workmanship?

4   It may be said that natural selection is daily and hourly scrutinising(仔细检查), throughout the world, every variation, even the slightest; rejecting that which is bad, preserving and adding up all that is good; silently and *insensibly* working, whenever and wherever opportunity offers, at the improvement of each organic being in relation to its organic and inorganic conditions of life. We see nothing of these slow changes in progress, until the hand of time has marked the long *lapses* of ages, and then so imperfect is our view into long past geological ages, that we only see that the forms of life are now different from what they formerly were.

5   We already see how it *entails* extinction; and how largely extinction has acted on the world's history, geology plainly declares. Natural selection, also, leads to divergence(分歧) of character; for more living beings can be supported on the same area the more they diverge in structure, habits, and constitution, of which we see proof by looking at the inhabitants of any small spot or at naturalised productions. Therefore during the modification of the *descendants* of any one species, and during the *incessant* struggle of all species to increase in numbers, the more *diversified* these descendants become, the better will be their chance of succeeding in the battle of life. Thus the small differences *distinguishing* varieties of the same species, will steadily tend to increase till they come to equal the greater differences between species of the same genus(类,种), or even of distinct genera.

New Words

potent	[ˈpəutənt]	a.	having great influence; powerful and effective 有效的; 有说服力的
peculiarity	[pi͵kju:liˈæriti]	n.	the quality of being peculiar to or characteristic of an individual person or thing; a distinguishing or special characteristic 特性; 特质
organic	[ɔːˈgænik]	a.	living, or produced by or from living things 有机的; 组织的
variation	[͵vɛəriˈeiʃən]	n.	a difference between similar things, or a change from the usual amount or form of something 变化; 差别
individual	[͵indiˈvidjuəl]	n.	a person, considered separately from the rest of the group or society that they live in 个人, 个体
rigidly	[ˈridʒidli]	ad.	in a stiff and strict manner 严格地; 坚硬地; 严厉地
fluctuate	[ˈflʌktjueit]	v.	to change, especially continuously and between one level or thing and another 波动; 涨落; 动摇
inhabitant	[inˈhæbitənt]	n.	a person or animal that lives in a particular place 居民; 居住者

Unit 7

immigrate	[ˈimigreit]	v.	to come to live in a different country 移入，使移居入境
mammal	[ˈmæməl]	n.	a type of animal that drinks milk from its mother's body when it is young 哺乳动物
modify	[ˈmɔdifai]	v.	to change sth. slightly, usually to improve it or make it more acceptable 修改，修饰；更改
intruder	[inˈtruːdə]	n.	someone who is in a place or situation where they are not wanted 侵入者；干扰者；妨碍者
arise	[əˈraiz]	v.	happen 出现
scope	[skəup]	n.	the range of a subject, opportunity 范围；机会
methodical	[miˈθɔdikəl]	a.	done in a very ordered, careful way 有系统的；有方法的；有条不紊的
constitutional	[ˌkɔnstiˈtjuːʃənl]	a.	allowed by or contained in a constitution; relating to someone's general state of health 宪法的；本质的；体质上的
vigorous	[ˈvigərəs]	a.	forceful or energetic 有力的；精力充沛的
prominent	[ˈprɔminənt]	a.	very well known and important 突出的，显著的；杰出的；卓越的
consequently	[ˈkɔnsiˌkwəntli]	ad.	as a result 结果
insensibly	[inˈsensəbli]	ad.	in a numb manner; without feeling 不知不觉地；徐徐地；极细微地
lapse	[læps]	n.	a period of time passing between two things happening 失效；流逝
entail	[inˈteil]	v.	involve sth. as a necessary part or result 必需；承担；蕴含
descendant	[diˈsendənt]	n.	a person considered as descended from some ancestor or race 后裔；子孙
incessant	[inˈsesənt]	a.	never stopping, especially in an annoying or unpleasant way 不断的；不停的；连续的
diversify	[daiˈvəːsifai]	v.	start to include more different types or things; vary 使多样化，使变化
distinguish	[disˈtiŋgwiʃ]	v.	notice or understand the difference between two things, or to make one person or thing seem different from another 区分；辨别；使杰出，使表现突出

bear in mind	remember; keep in mind 记住；考虑到
have advantage(s) over	be superior to 比……有优势
fill up	make full 填补；装满；堵塞
in the course of	in process of 在……过程中；在……期间
except in so far as	except; apart from 除去
catch one's eye	draw one's attention 引人注目

1. The text was adapted from *Natural Selection* by Charles Darwin.
2. The author of the book, Charles Robert Darwin, (12 February, 1809—19 April, 1882) was an English naturalist and geologist, best known for his contributions to evolutionary theory. He established that all species of life have descended over time from common ancestors, and in a joint publication with Alfred Russel Wallace introduced his scientific theory that this branching pattern of evolution resulted from a process that he called natural selection, in which the struggle for existence has a similar effect to the artificial selection involved in selective breeding. Darwin published his theory of evolution with compelling evidence in his 1859 book *On the Origin of Species,* overcoming scientific rejection of earlier concepts of transmutation of species.

Task 1   Generating the Outline

Directions: Please identify the thesis of the passage and the main point of each paragraph and find out how these points develop the thesis. You may use the table below to help you.

The thesis	The principle of selection can apply both in _____.
Para. 1: The problem	Can _____ be affected by natural selection?
Para. 2: The Answer	_____ would most seriously affect many of the others.
Para. 3: Comparison	_____ should be far "truer" in character than man's production.
Para. 4: Conclusion	Natural selection is daily and hourly _____; _____, _____ and _____; silently and insensibly _____.
Para. 5: The effect	_____ will steadily tend to increase till they come to equal the greater differences between _____.

Task 2   Understanding the Text

Directions: Please answer the following ten questions based on Text A.

1. Would Darwin believe the principle of selection can apply in nature? Why or why not?

2. How can "the mutual relations of all organic beings to each other and to their physical conditions of life" be described?
3. In what conditions can we doubt that individuals having any advantages over others would have the best chance of surviving and of procreating their kind?
4. What would be left a fluctuating element?
5. What can we conclude from what we have seen of the intimate and complex manner in which the inhabitants of each country are bound together?
6. In what cases would every slight modification tend to be preserved?
7. Who can act on every internal organ, and by whom can selected character by fully exercised?
8. What would nature's products be like, compared with those of man during the whole geological periods?
9. What is the natural selection doing daily and hourly, silently and insensibly?
10. According to the article, what would the small differences distinguishing varieties of the same species tend to do?

Task 3 Vocabulary Building

Directions: Conversion is a word-formation process whereby a word of certain word-class is shifted into a word of another word-class without an addition of an affix, which is also called "functional shift" or "derivation by zero suffix". For example:

For example, the verb "*struggle*" in Paragraph 3 "He does not allow the most vigorous males to struggle for the females." can be derived to be the noun "struggle" in the sentence in Paragraph 5 "... and during the incessant struggle of all species to increase in numbers..."

Please fill in the blanks with the proper word form:

bear

1. A _____ is a large, strong wild animal with thick fur and sharp claws.
2. Let it _____ in mind how infinitely complex and close-fitting are the mutual relations of all organic beings to each other and ... (Para.1)
3. The strain must have been enormous but she _____ it well.

influence

1. Let it be remembered how powerful the _____ of a single introduced tree or mammal has been shown to be. (Para.2)
2. The result would _____ by various factors.

mark

1. Wealth was the _____ of success or failure in that society.
2. We see nothing of these slow changes in progress, until the hand of time has _____ the long lapses of ages... (Para.4)

place

1. You can put those tools in the right _____.
2. The series of unprecedented accidents have _____ the boy under serious fright.

Task 4 Learning the Phrases

Directions: Please fill in the blanks in the sentences below with the phrases listed in the box. Change the forms if necessary. Notice that some phrases need to be used more than once.

| bear in mind | bear the stamp of | except in so far as |
| have advantage over | in the course of | catch one's eye |

1. Their paintings _____ sufferings in the second world war.
2. In none of these respects does optical astronomy _____ any _____ radio astronomy.
3. It must _____ that all souls are following a path that they have chosen for themselves.
4. They thought of the individual as completely lacking in significance _____ he could come up with some good ideas.
5. You should _____ that all figures published in the media are only the figures for the dead.
6. He also believed that human beings have responsibility to protect the planet _____ human events.
7. One natural reason children have become valuable tools to _____ nation's _____ is that, as those economists predicted, children are the main source of opening pocketbooks.
8. _____ his research, he became extremely keen on the evolution of this species.

Task 5 Studying the Sentence Structure

Sentences with it-extraposition

Sentences from the text

1. Let it be borne in mind in what an endless number of strange peculiarities our domestic productions... (Para. 1)
2. Let it be borne in mind how infinitely complex and close-fitting are the mutual relations of all organic beings to each other and to their physical conditions of life. (Para. 1)
3. Let it be remembered how powerful the influence of a single introduced tree or mammal has been shown to be. (Para. 2)

Directions: Please follow the examples and create five sentences on your own.

Tips

1. Extraposition is a mechanism of syntax that alters word order in such a manner that a relatively "heavy" constituent appears to the right of its canonical position. The term "extraposition" is also used to denote similar structures in which *it* appears.
2. In cases of *it-extraposition*, extraposition is not optional, but rather it is obligatory.

3. It-extraposition that distinguishes it from canonical cases is that the extraposed constituent is usually a clause. In other words, *It* is pro-form of a sort; its appearance pushes the clause that it stands for to the end of the sentence.
4. It-extraposition cannot extrapose a prepositional phrase.

1. _____
   _____.
2. _____
   _____.
3. _____
   _____.
4. _____
   _____.
5. _____
   _____.

Task 6 Paraphrasing Difficult Sentences

1. Can it, then, be thought improbable, seeing that variations useful to man have undoubtedly occurred, that other variations useful in some way to each being in the great and complex battle of life, should sometimes occur in the course of thousands of generations?
   _____
   _____.

2. We may conclude, from what we have seen of the intimate and complex manner in which the inhabitants of each country are bound together, that any change in the numerical proportions of some of the inhabitants, independently of the change of climate itself, would most seriously affect many of the others.
   _____
   _____.

3. In such cases, every slight modification, which in the course of ages chanced to arise, and which in any way favoured the individuals of any of the species, by better adapting them to their altered conditions, would tend to be preserved; and natural selection would thus have free scope for the work of improvement.
   _____
   _____.

4. Can we wonder, then, that nature's productions should be far "truer" in character than man's productions; that they should be infinitely better adapted to the most complex conditions of life, and should plainly bear the stamp of far higher workmanship?
   _____
   _____.

5. It may be said that natural selection is daily and hourly scrutinising, throughout the world, every variation, even the slightest; rejecting that which is bad, preserving and adding up all that is good; silently and insendibly working, whenever and wherever opportunity offers, at the improvement of

each organic being in relation to its organic and inorganic conditions of life.

_____
_____.

6. We see nothing of these slow changes in progress, until the hand of time has marked the long lapses of ages, and then so imperfect is our view into long past geological ages, that we only see that the forms of life are now different from what they formerly were.

_____
_____.

7. Therefore during the modification of the descendants of any one species, and during the incessant struggle of all species to increase in numbers, the more diversified these descendants become, the better will be their chance of succeeding in the battle of life.

_____
_____.

8. Thus the small differences distinguishing varieties of the same species, will steadily tend to increase till they come to equal the greater differences between species of the same genus, or even of distinct genera.

_____
_____.

Task 7 Summarizing the Text

Directions: Please summarize Text A in 100 words. You may use the table in Task 1 to help you.

Task 8 Writing with Cause and Effect

Directions: write a passage to discuss the effects of natural selection on the world. You should try to clearly analyze the cause and the effect. You may use what is provided in the box below to help you, especially those in italics to indicate the cause and effect.

Tips

1. The cause-effect essay you write will depend on the topic you choose and the main point you wish to communicate. If, for example, your purpose is to tell readers about the impact natural selection had on the world, the essay would mainly focus on the effects. However, if your purpose is to explain why the world has been affected by the natural selection, the essay would focus on the causes.

2. As with all essays, try to pick a topic that will appeal to your readers. In addition to selecting a lively topic, be sure to make your main point clear so that your readers can follow the cause-effect relationship you have developed. You'd better announce specific causes and effects by signaling them to readers.

1. Natural selection is the gradual process by which heritable biological traits *become* either more or less common in a population as a function of *the effect of* inherited traits on the differential reproductive success of organisms interacting with their environment.
2. Variation occurs *partly because* random mutations arise in the genome of an individual organism, and these mutations can be passed to offspring.
3. Throughout the individuals' lives, their genomes interact with their environments to *cause* variations in traits.
4. Individuals with certain variants of the trait may survive and reproduce more than individuals with other, less successful, variants. *Therefore* the population evolves.
5. Natural selection is *one of the cornerstones* of modern biology.
6. The phenotype is the result of the genotype and the environment in which the organism lives.
7. Pollution has been found to be present widely in the environment. There are a number of *effects* of this.
8. Carbon dioxide emissions *cause* ocean acidification, the ongoing decrease in the PH of the Earth's oceans as CO_2 becomes dissolved.
9. The emission of greenhouse gases *leads to* global warming which *affects* ecosystems in many ways.
10. Invasive species *can out compete* native species and reduce biodiversity. Invasive plants can *contribute* debris and biomolecules (allelopathy) that *can alter* soil and chemical compositions of an environment, *often reducing* native species competitiveness.
11. Nitrogen oxides are removed from the air by rain and fertilise land which *can change* the species composition of ecosystems.
12. Smog and haze *can reduce* the amount of sunlight received by plants to carry out photosynthesis and leads to the production of tropospheric ozone which *damages* plants.
13. Soil *can become* infertile and unsuitable for plants. This will *affect* other organisms in the food web.
14. Sulfur dioxide and nitrogen oxides can cause acid rain which lowers the PH value of soil.

Part Three   Reading and Speaking

Text B

Nature
Emerson

1   To go into *solitude*, a man needs to retire as much from his *chamber* as from society. I am not solitary whilst I read and write, though nobody is with me. But if a man would be alone, let him look at the stars. The rays that come from those heavenly

worlds, will separate between him and what he touches. One might think the atmosphere was made transparent with this design, to give man, in the heavenly bodies, the *perpetual* presence of the *sublime*. Seen in the streets of cities, how great they are! If the stars should appear one night in a thousand years, how would men believe and *adore*; and preserve for many generations the remembrance of the city of God which had been shown! But every night come out these envoys of beauty, and light the universe with their admonishing smile.

2   The stars awaken a certain reverence, because though always present, they are *inaccessible*; but all natural objects make a kindred impression, when the mind is open to their influence. Nature never wears a mean appearance. Neither does the wisest man extort her secret, and lose his curiosity by finding out all her perfection. Nature never became a toy to a wise spirit. The flowers, the animals, the mountains, reflected the wisdom of his best hour, as much as they had delighted the simplicity of his childhood.

3   When we speak of nature in this manner, we have a distinct but most poetical sense in the mind. We mean the *integrity* of impression made by *manifold* natural objects. It is this which distinguishes the stick of timber of the wood-cutter, from the tree of the poet. The charming landscape which I saw this morning, is indubitably made up of some twenty or thirty farms. Miller owns this field, Locke that, and Manning the woodland beyond. But none of them owns the landscape. There is a property in the horizon which no man has but he whose eye can integrate all the parts, that is, the poet. This is the best part of these men's farms, yet to this their warranty-deeds give no title.

4   To speak truly, few adult persons can see nature. Most persons do not see the sun. At least they have a very superficial seeing. The sun *illuminates* only the eye of the man, but shines into the eye and the heart of the child. The lover of nature is he whose inward and outward senses are still truly adjusted to each other; who has retained the spirit of infancy even into the era of manhood. His *intercourse* with heaven and earth, becomes part of his daily food. *In the presence of* nature, a wild delight *runs through* the man, in spite of real sorrows. Nature says, —he is my creature, and maugre (不管) all his impertinent griefs, he shall be glad with me. Not the sun or the summer alone, but every hour and season yields its *tribute* of delight; for every hour and change *corresponds to* and authorizes a different state of the mind, from breathless noon to grimmest midnight. Nature is a setting that fits equally well a comic or a mourning piece. In good health, the air is a *cordial* of incredible virtue. Crossing a bare common, in snow puddles, at *twilight*, under a clouded sky, without having in my thoughts any occurrence of special good fortune, I have enjoyed a perfect exhilaration. I am glad to the *brink* of fear. In the woods too, a man casts off his years, as the snake his slough, and at what period so ever of life, is always a child. In the woods, is perpetual youth. Within these plantations of God, a decorum and sanctity *reign*, a perennial festival is dressed, and the guest sees not how he should tire of them in a thousand years. In

the woods, we return to reason and faith. There I feel that nothing can befall me in life, —no disgrace, no *calamity*, (leaving me my eyes,) which nature cannot repair. Standing on the bare ground, —my head bathed by the blithe(愉快无忧的) air, and uplifted into infinite space, —all mean egotism vanishes. I become a transparent eye-ball; I am nothing; I see all; the currents of the Universal Being circulate through me; I am part or particle of God. The name of the nearest friend sounds then foreign and accidental: to be brothers, to be *acquaintances*, —master or servant, is then a trifle and a disturbance. I am the lover of uncontained and immortal beauty. In the wilderness, I find something more dear and connate than in streets or villages. In the *tranquil* landscape, and especially in the distant line of the horizon, man beholds somewhat as beautiful as his own nature.

5   The greatest delight which the fields and woods minister, is the suggestion of an occult(神秘的) relation between man and the vegetable. I am not alone and unacknowledged. They nod to me, and I to them. The waving of the boughs in the storm, is new to me and old. It takes me by surprise, and yet is not unknown. Its effect is like that of a higher thought or a better emotion coming over me, when I deemed I was thinking justly or doing right.

6   Yet it is certain that the power to produce this delight, does not *reside* in nature, but in man, or in a harmony of both. It is necessary to use these pleasures with great temperance. For, nature is not always tricked in holiday attire, but the same scene which yesterday breathed perfume and *glittered* as for the *frolic* of the *nymphs*, is overspread with *melancholy* today. Nature always wears the colors of the spirit. To a man laboring under calamity, the heat of his own fire hath sadness in it. Then, there is a kind of contempt of the landscape felt by him who has just lost by death a dear friend. The sky is less grand as it shuts down over less worth in the population.

New Words

solitude	[ˈsɔlitjuːd]	n.	the situation of being alone without other people 孤独；隐居
chamber	[ˈtʃeimbə]	n.	a room used for a special or official purpose 房间；会所
perpetual	[pəˈpetʃuəl]	a.	continuing forever or indefinitely 永久的；不断的
sublime	[səˈblaim]	n.	sth. that is so good or beautiful that you are deeply affected by it 崇高；顶点
adore	[əˈdɔː]	v.	love someone very much and feel very proud of them 崇拜；爱慕

inaccessible	[ˌinækˈsesəbl]	a.	very difficult or impossible to travel to 难达到的, 难接近的
integrity	[inˈtegrəti]	n.	the quality of being honest and strong about what you believe to be right 正直, 诚实
manifold	[ˈmænɪfəʊld]	a.	of many different kinds 各种各样的, 多样的
illuminate	[iˈlju:mineit]	v.	to explain and show more clearly sth. that is difficult to understand; to light sth. and make it brighter 阐明, 说明; 照亮; 使灿烂
intercourse	[ˈintəkɔ:s]	n.	conversation and social activity between people 交往, 交流
tribute	[ˈtrɪbju:t]	n.	sth. that you say, write or give which shows your respect and admiration for someone, especially on a formal occasion 颂词, 礼物; 致敬, 悼念
cordial	[ˈkɔ:djəl]	a.	friendly, but formal and polite 热忱的, 诚恳的
twilight	[ˈtwailait]	n.	the period just before it becomes completely dark in the evening 黄昏; 薄暮
occurrence	[əˈkə:rəns]	n.	sth. that happens 发生; 出现; 事件
brink	[brɪŋk]	n.	the point where a new or different situation is about to begin; the edge of a cliff or other high area (峭壁的)边缘
reign	[reɪn]	v.	to be the main feeling or quality in a situation or person 统治; 支配; 盛行
calamity	[kəˈlæmɪtɪ]	n.	a serious accident or bad event causing damage or suffering 灾难; 不幸事件
circulate	[ˈsɜ:kjʊleɪt]	v.	to go around or through sth., or to make sth. go around or through sth. 传播, 流传; 循环; 流通
acquaintance	[əˈkweɪntəns]	n.	a person that you have met but do not know well 熟人, 相识
tranquil	[ˈtræŋkwɪl]	a.	calm and peaceful and without noise, violence, worry, etc. 安静的, 平静的; 安宁的
reside	[rɪˈzaɪd]	v.	to live, have your home, or stay in a place 住, 居住
glitter	[ˈglɪtə]	v.	to produce a lot of small bright flashes of reflected light 闪光, 闪烁
frolic	[ˈfrɒlɪk]	n.	happy behaviour, like that of children playing 嬉闹, 嬉戏
nymph	[nɪmf]	n.	(in ancient Greek and Roman traditional stories) a goddess or spirit in the form of a young woman, living in a tree, river, mountain, etc. 宁芙; 希腊和罗马神话中的自然女神, 常常化身为年轻女子

Unit 7

| melancholy | ['melənkəlı] | n. | sadness that lasts for a long period of time, often without any obvious reason 忧郁；悲哀 |

in the presence of	in the face of 在……面前
run through	go quickly through 跑着穿过；浏览；刺
correspond to	to match or be similar or equal 相当于……，符合于……

1. This passage was adapted from *Nature* by Ralph Waldo Emerson.
2. The author Ralph Waldo Emerson (May 25, 1803—April 27, 1882) was an American essayist, lecturer, and poet, who led the Transcendentalist movement of the mid-19th century. He was seen as a champion of individualism and a prescient critic of the countervailing pressures of society, and he disseminated his thoughts through dozens of published essays and more than 1,500 public lectures across the United States. Emerson gradually moved away from the religious and social beliefs of his contemporaries, formulating and expressing the philosophy of Transcendentalism in his 1836 essay, Nature. Emerson wrote most of his important essays as lectures first, then revised them for print. His first two collections of essays—*Essays: First Series* and *Essays: Second Series,* published respectively in 1841 and 1844—represent the core of his thinking, and include such well-known essays as *Self-Reliance*, *The Over-Soul*, *Circles*, *The Poet* and *Experience*. Together with *Nature*, these essays made the decade from the mid-1830s to the mid-1840s Emerson's most fertile period.

Task 1 Summarizing

Directions: Fill in the blanks in the following text outline with key points based on an overall understanding and then make an oral summary.

I. The beauty of nature
   a. To go into solitude, _____.
   b. Stars are _____—
   c. The poetic sense in mind means _____.

II. The relations between man and nature
   a. _____ can see nature
   b. The greatest delight is _____.
   c. The power to make this delight _____.

Task 2　Reflections on the text

Directions: After reading the above text, you can discuss the passage with your partners and then give an oral presentation of your reflections on the text.

Guiding Questions：

1. Can you define the beauty of nature?
2. What makes nature so charming?
3. How can you enjoy delight from nature?
4. What is the relation between man and nature?
5. What is more important, the economic development or the nature conservation?

Task 3　Making a Presentation

Directions: Please give an oral presentation of your views on the following topics. You should first state your view clearly and then support your view with details.

Topics:

1. The beauty of nature
2. The impact of human behavior on nature

Below are some expressions that you might find useful in your presentation.

> 1) the masterpiece of God
> 2) the graces of the winter scenery
> 3) natural resources
> 4) the earth's ecosystem
> 5) natural disasters like tsunami, blizzard, hurricane, earthquake, flood and drought, etc.
> 6) global warming
> 7) melting polar caps
> 8) poisonous pollutant
> 9) coexist in harmony
> 10) peaceful and harmonious world with love and warmth

Part Four　Cross Cultural Communication

Passage A

老子的智慧

林语堂

　　老子的隽语，像粉碎的宝石，不需装饰便可自闪光耀。然而，人们心灵渴求的却是更深一层的理解，于是，老子这谜般的智慧宝石，便传到变化繁杂的注释者手中。甚至在我国，许多学者将它译给与本国思想、观念完全不同的另一个世界——英语世界。

老子爱唱反调,几成怪癖。"无为而无不为""圣人非以其无私,故能成其私",这种反论的结构恰如水晶之形成:把某一物质的温度改变,即成水晶,但成品却是许许多多的水晶体。

一件事理的基本观点和价值,与另一种普遍为人接受的观点完全相反时,便产生了反面论。耶稣的反论是:"失去生命者,获得生命。"这种反论的起因,乃是把两类特殊的生命观(精神与肉体)融而为一,呈现在表面的,就是反面论。

到底什么思想使老子产生了那么多强调柔弱的力量、居下的优势和对成功的警戒等反面论呢?答案是:宇宙周而复始的学说——所谓生命,乃是一种不断地变迁,交互兴盛和腐败的现象,当一个人的生命力达到巅峰时,也正象征着要开始走下坡了;犹如潮水的消长,潮水退尽,接着开始涨潮。

老子说:"心困焉而不能知,口辟焉而不能言,尝为女议乎其将。至阴肃肃,至阳赫赫,肃肃出乎天,赫赫发乎地;两者交通成和,而无生焉。或为之纪,而莫见其形;消息满虚,一晦一明,日改月化,日有所为,而莫见其功。生有所乎萌,死有所乎归,始终相反乎无端,而莫知其所穷。非是也,且孰为之宗。"

另外一种研究老子之法,乃从爱默生的短文《循环论》着手。这篇文章的观点,基于道家思想,爱默生运用诗歌顿呼语"循环哲学家"中之"循环",导出了与老子同样的思想体系。

爱默生强调:"终即始;黑夜之后必有黎明;大洋之下另有深渊。"惠施亦言:"日方中方睨。"另外,庄子也说道:"在太极之先,而不为高;在六极之下,而不为深。"爱默生更谈到:"自然无定""人亦无定";所以,"新大陆建于旧行星的毁灭,新种族兴于祖先的腐朽"。

从这些循环论,爱默生发展了一套类似老子的反论:"最精明即最不精明","社会的道德乃圣者之恶","人渴望安定,却得不到安定",读者可在庄子的精选中,发现爱默生的这种论点。

由此可知,爱默生的两篇短文《循环论》及《超灵论》,和道家的主张确有异曲同工之妙,看过《老子》一书后,读者自可体会出其中滋味。爱默生对相对论深信不疑,他曾说:"一人的美是另一人的丑;一人之智慧是另一人的愚蠢。"且引用美国北佬农夫常说的典型道家谚语:"不必祝福,事情愈坏,情况愈好。"

以哲学观点而论,"道"可概括如下:它是天地万物的主要单元(一元论),是"反面立论""阴阳两极""永久循环""相对论""本体论"的主体;它是神智,是复归为一和万物的源泉。

 Notes

1. 这篇文章节选自林语堂《老子的智慧》。此书是林语堂向西方介绍道家乃至整个中国古代哲学思想的一部重要著作。全书阐释了老子思想的独特性、道家哲学与儒家哲学的不同、并强调要结合庄子研究老子。
2. 作者林语堂福建龙溪(漳州)人,1895年10月10日出生,1976年3月26日逝世。中国现当代著名文学家,原名和乐,改名玉堂、语堂,笔名毛驴、宰予、岂青等。早年留学国外,回国后在北京大学等著名大学任教,1966年定居台湾。他的一生著述颇丰,在文学、语言学、历史和中外文化交流等众多领域都取得了巨大成就,是著名作家、学者、翻译家。曾先后出席国际大学校长协会、国际笔会大会等重要会议,被推举为国际笔会副会长,并因《京华烟云》一书被提名诺贝尔文学奖候选人。

Word Bank

无为而无不为	Do nothing and everything is done.
反面立论	reversion
至阴肃肃,至阳赫赫	The great yin is majestically silent; the great yang is impressively active.
日方中方睨	When the sun is at its zenith, it is setting somewhere else.
消息满虚	Growth alternates with decay
阴阳两极	polarization(yin and yang)
一元论	monism
复归为一	the return of all to the Primeval One

Directions: Please summarize the passage in English. Your summary should be about 150—200 words.

Passage B

Remarks at Paris Summit on Climate Change

Barack Obama

President Hollande, Mr. Secretary General, fellow leaders. We have come to Paris to show our resolve.

We offer our condolences to the people of France for the barbaric attacks on this beautiful city. We stand united in solidarity not only to deliver justice to the terrorist network responsible for those attacks but to protect our people and uphold the enduring values that keep us strong and keep us free. And we salute the people of Paris for insisting this crucial conference go on—an act of defiance that proves nothing will deter us from building the future we want for our children. What greater rejection of those who would tear down our world than marshaling our best efforts to save it?

Nearly 200 nations have assembled here this week—a declaration that for all the challenges we face, the growing threat of climate change could define the contours of this century more dramatically than any other. What should give us hope that this is a turning point, that this is the moment we finally determined we would save our planet, is the fact that our nations share a sense of urgency about this challenge and a growing realization that it is within our power to do something about it.

Our understanding of the ways human beings disrupt the climate advances by the day. Fourteen of the fifteen warmest years on record have occurred since the year 2000—and 2015 is on pace to be the warmest year of all. No nation—large or small, wealthy or poor—is immune to what this means.

This summer, I saw the effects of climate change firsthand in our northernmost state, Alaska, where the sea is already swallowing villages and eroding shorelines; where permafrost thaws and the tundra burns; where glaciers are melting at a pace unprecedented in modern times. And it was a preview of one possible future—a glimpse of our children's fate if the climate keeps changing faster than our efforts to address it. Submerged countries. Abandoned cities. Fields that no longer grow. Political disruptions that trigger new conflict, and even more floods of desperate peoples seeking the sanctuary of nations not their own.

That future is not one of strong economies, nor is it one where fragile states can find their footing. That future is one that we have the power to change. Right here. Right now. But only if we rise to this moment. As one of America's governors has said, "We are the first generation to feel the impact of climate change, and the last generation that can do something about it."

I've come here personally, as the leader of the world's largest economy and the second-largest emitter, to say that the United States of America not only recognizes our role in creating this problem, we embrace our responsibility to do something about it.

Over the last seven years, we've made ambitious investments in clean energy, and ambitious reductions in our carbon emissions. We've multiplied wind power threefold, and solar power more than twentyfold, helping create parts of America where these clean power sources are finally cheaper than dirtier, conventional power. We've invested in energy efficiency in every way imaginable. We've said no to infrastructure that would pull high-carbon fossil fuels from the ground, and we've said yes to the first-ever set of national standards limiting the amount of carbon pollution our power plants can release into the sky.

The advances we've made have helped drive our economic output to all-time highs, and drive our carbon pollution to its lowest levels in nearly two decades.

But the good news is this is not an American trend alone. Last year, the global economy grew while global carbon emissions from burning fossil fuels stayed flat. And what this means can't be overstated. We have broken the old arguments for inaction. We have proved that strong economic growth and a safer environment no longer have to conflict with one another; they can work in concert with one another.

And that should give us hope. One of the enemies that we'll be fighting at this conference is cynicism, the notion we can't do anything about climate change. Our progress should give us hope during these two weeks—hope that is rooted in collective action.

Earlier this month in Dubai, after years of delay, the world agreed to work together to cut the super-pollutants known as HFCs. That's progress. Already, prior to Paris, more than 180 countries representing nearly 95 percent of global emissions have put forward their own climate targets. That is progress. For our part, America is on track to reach the emissions targets that I set six years ago in Copenhagen—we will reduce our carbon emissions in the range of 17 percent below 2005 levels by 2020. And that's why, last year, I set a new target: America will reduce our emissions 26 to 28 percent below 2005 levels within 10 years from now.

So our task here in Paris is to turn these achievements into an enduring framework for human progress—not a stopgap solution, but a long-term strategy that gives the world confidence in a low-carbon future.

Here, in Paris, let's secure an agreement that builds in ambition, where progress paves the way for regularly updated targets—targets that are not set for each of us but by each of us, taking into account the differences that each nation is facing.

Here in Paris, let's agree to a strong system of transparency that gives each of us the confidence that all of us are meeting our commitments. And let's make sure that the countries who don't yet have the full capacity to report on their targets receive the support that they need.

Here in Paris, let's reaffirm our commitment that resources will be there for countries willing to do their part to skip the dirty phase of development. And I recognize this will not be easy. It will take a commitment to innovation and the capital to continue driving down the cost of clean energy. And that's why, this afternoon, I'll join many of you to announce an historic joint effort to accelerate public and private clean energy innovation on a global scale.

Here in Paris, let's also make sure that these resources flow to the countries that need help preparing for the impacts of climate change that we can no longer avoid. We know the truth that many nations have contributed little to climate change but will be the first to feel its most destructive effects. For some, particularly island nations—whose leaders I'll meet with tomorrow—climate change is a threat to their very existence. And that's why today, in concert with other nations, America confirms our strong and ongoing commitment to the Least Developed Countries Fund. And tomorrow, we'll pledge new contributions to risk insurance initiatives that help vulnerable populations rebuild stronger after climate-related disasters.

And finally, here in Paris, let's show businesses and investors that the global economy is on a firm path towards a low-carbon future. If we put the right rules and incentives in place, we'll unleash the creative power of our best scientists and engineers and entrepreneurs to deploy clean energy technologies and the new jobs and new opportunities that they create all around the world. There are hundreds of billions of dollars ready to deploy to countries around the world if they get the signal that we mean business this time. Let's send that signal.

That's what we seek in these next two weeks. Not simply an agreement to roll back the pollution we put into our skies, but an agreement that helps us lift people from poverty without condemning the next generation to a planet that's beyond its capacity to repair. Here, in Paris, we can show the world what is possible when we come together, united in common effort and by a common purpose.

And let there be no doubt, the next generation is watching what we do. Just over a week ago, I was in Malaysia, where I held a town hall with young people, and the first question I received was from a young Indonesian woman. And it wasn't about terrorism, it wasn't about the economy, it wasn't about human rights. It was about climate change. And she asked whether I was optimistic about what we can achieve here in Paris, and what young people like her could do to help.

I want our actions to show her that we're listening. I want our actions to be big enough to draw on the talents of all our people—men and women, rich and poor—I want to show her passionate, idealistic young generation that we care about their future.

For I believe, in the words of Dr. Martin Luther King, Jr., that there is such a thing as being too late. And when it comes to climate change, that hour is almost upon us. But if we act here, if we act now, if we place our own short-term interests behind the air that our young people will breathe, and the food that they will eat, and the water that they will drink, and the hopes and dreams that sustain their lives, then we won't be too late for them.

And, my fellow leaders, accepting this challenge will not reward us with moments of victory that are clear or quick. Our progress will be measured differently—in the suffering that is averted, and a planet that's preserved. And that's what's always made this so hard. Our generation may not even live to see the full realization of what we do here. But the knowledge that the next generation will be better off for what we do here—can we imagine a more worthy reward than that? Passing that on to our children and our grandchildren, so that when they look back and they see what we did here in Paris, they can take pride in our achievement.

Let that be the common purpose here in Paris. A world that is worthy of our children. A world that is marked not by conflict, but by cooperation; and not by human suffering, but by human progress. A world that's safer, and more prosperous, and more secure, and more free than the one that we inherited.

Let's get to work. Thank you very much.

 **Notes**

1. The passage was adapted from *Remarks at Paris Summit on Climate Change*.
2. Barack Obama is the 44th and current President of the United States, and the first African American to hold the office.
3. The 2015 United Nations Climate Change Conference, commonly known as the Paris Summit, was held between 30 November and 11 December. US President Barack Obama was one of 147 world leaders to address delegates in Paris on 30 November at the opening of the United Nations Conference on Climate Change (COP21). The United States is the world's second-largest emitter of greenhouse gases after China.

Directions: Please summarize the passage in Chinese. Your summary should be about 200—300 words.

Unit 8

SCIENCE AND EDUCATION

If scientific education is to be dealt with as mere bookwork, it will be better not to attempt it, but to stick to the Latin Grammar which makes no pretense to be anything but bookwork.

—*From Scientific Education by Thomas Henry Huxley*

But if we join them, are we still human? Or will we become the creatures we have for so long feared and so far only fictionalized: superior beings who see organic, naturally born humans as ill-equipped competition?

—*From Man or Machine by Andrew Belonsky*

Learning Objectives

Upon the completion of this unit, you should be able to

Remembering & Understanding	★ read Text A and Text B aloud smoothly with expression indicative of comprehension and tone; ★ identify and explain in your own words the thesis and the major points of Text A and Text B;
Analyzing & Applying	★ make reference to the thesis and/or the major points of Text A and Text B in your writing; ★ produce sentences with adverbial clauses of concession and result; ★ use parallel sentences for rhetoric effect;
Evaluating & Creating	★ adopt relevant writing strategies in cause-and-effect paragraphs; ★ participate in the discussion by expressing your own ideas based on your reflection on Text A and Text B; ★ deliver a clear and coherent presentation of your views on the topics centering on the relationship between man and machine.

Unit 8

Part One Lead-in

Section 1 Listening: Technology Abuse

Task 1 Filling the Blanks

Directions: Please fill in the blanks with one or two words on the basis of what you have heard.

  Yes, these technologies will be abused. However, an outright ban, in my view, would be _____, morally indefensible, and in any event would not address the dangers. Nanotechnology, for example, is not a specific well-defined field. It is simply the _____ end-result of the trend toward miniaturization which permeates virtually all technology. We've all seen _____ miniaturization in our lifetimes. Technology in all forms—electronic, _____, biological, and others—is shrinking, currently at a rate of 5.6 per linear dimension per decade. The inescapable result will be nanotechnology. With regard to more intelligent computers and software, it's an inescapable economic _____ affecting every company from large firms like Sun and Microsoft to small _____ companies. With regard to biotechnology, are we going to tell the many millions of cancer sufferers around the world that although we are on the verge of new treatments that may save their lives, we're nonetheless canceling all of this research? Banning these new technologies would _____ not just millions, but billions of people to the anguish of disease and poverty that we would otherwise be able to _____. And attempting to ban these technologies won't even eliminate the danger because it will only push these technologies underground where development would continue _____ by ethics and regulation. We often go through three stages in examining the impact of future technology: awe and wonderment at its _____ to overcome age-old problems, then a sense of dread at a new set of grave dangers that accompany these new technologies, followed by the realization that the only viable and responsible path is to set a careful course that can realize the promise while managing the peril. The only viable approach is a combination of strong ethical standards, _____ law enforcement, and, most importantly, the development of both technical safeguards and technological immune systems to combat specific dangers.

Task 2 Group Discussion

Directions: Please discuss the following questions in pairs or groups based on what you have heard.

1. According to the speaker, how pervasive is miniaturization in our lifetimes?
2. What will be the consequence of attempting to ban new technologies such as biotechnology?
3. How should we combat specific dangers that accompany those new technologies?

Section 2 Watching: Technology's Epic Story

Task 1 Group Discussion

Directions: Please watch the video "Technology's Epic Story" and discuss the three questions below in pairs or groups.

1. What does the speaker think of the default position about the emergence of a new technology?
2. How does the speaker understand the precautionary principle confronting a new technology?
3. What does technology give you? Try to use your own experience to illustrate your points of view.

Task 2 Summarizing

Directions: Please watch the video again, and try to summarize the speaker's attitude toward the relationship between humans and technology.

Part Two Reading and Writing

Text A

Scientific Education
Thomas Henry Huxley

1   I hope you will consider that the arguments I have now stated, even if there were no better ones, *constitute* a sufficient apology for *urging* the introduction of science into schools. The next question to which I have to address myself is, what sciences ought to be thus taught?

2   By this, however, I do not mean that every schoolboy should be taught everything in science. That would be a very absurd thing to *conceive*, and a very *mischievous* thing to attempt. What I mean is, that no boy nor girl should leave school without *possessing* a grasp of the general character of science, and without having been *disciplined*, more or less, in the methods of all sciences; so that, when turned into the world to make their own way, they shall be prepared to face scientific problems, not by knowing at once the conditions of every problem, or by being able at once to solve it; but by being familiar with the general current of scientific thought, and by being able to apply the methods of science in the proper way, when they have *acquainted* themselves with the conditions of the special problem.

3   I conceive the proper course to be somewhat as follows. To begin with, let every child be instructed in those general views of the phenomena of Nature for which we have no exact English name. The nearest *approximation* to a name for what I mean which we possess, is "physical geography." The Germans have a better, "Erdkunde" ("earth knowledge" or "*geology*" in its etymological sense) that is to say, a general knowledge of the earth, and what is on it, in it, and about it.

Unit 8

4 After this *preliminary* opening of the eyes to the great spectacle of the daily progress of Nature, as the reasoning *faculties* of the child grow, and he becomes familiar with the use of the tools of knowledge—reading, writing, and *elementary* mathematics—he should *pass on* to what is, in the more strict sense, physical science. Now there are two kinds of physical science: the one regards form and the relation of forms to one another; the other deals with causes and effects. In many of what we term sciences, these two kinds *are mixed up* together; but *systematic* botany is a pure example of the former kind, and physics of the latter kind, of science.

5 So far as school education is concerned, I want to go no further just now; and I believe that such instruction would make an excellent introduction to that preparatory scientific training which, as I have indicated, is so essential for the successful pursuit of our most important professions. But this modicum (少量) of instruction must be so given as to ensure real knowledge and practical discipline. If scientific education is to be dealt with as mere bookwork, it will be better not to attempt it, but to stick to the Latin Grammar which makes no *pretense* to be anything but bookwork.

6 If the great benefits of scientific training are sought, it is essential that such training should be real: that is to say, that the mind of the scholar should be brought into direct relation with fact, that he should not merely be told a thing, but made to see by the use of his own intellect and ability that the thing is so and no otherwise. The great *peculiarity* of scientific training, that *in virtue of* which it cannot be replaced by any other discipline whatsoever, is this bringing of the mind directly into contact with fact, and practicing the intellect in the completest form of induction; that is to say, in drawing conclusions from particular facts made known by immediate observation of Nature.

7 In all these respects, science differs from other educational discipline, and prepares the scholar for common life. What have we to do in every-day life? Most of the business which demands our attention is matter of fact, which needs, in the first place, to be accurately observed or *apprehended*; in the second, to be interpreted by *inductive* and *deductive* reasoning, which are altogether similar in their nature to those employed in science. In the one case, as in the other, whatever is taken for granted is so taken *at one's own peril*; fact and reason are the *ultimate* arbiters, and patience and honesty are the great helpers out of difficulty.

8 But if scientific training is to *yield* its most *eminent* results, it must, I repeat, be made practical. That is to say, in explaining to a child the general phenomena of Nature, you must, as far as possible, give reality to your teaching by object-lessons; in teaching him botany, he must handle the plants and dissect the flowers for himself; in teaching him physics and chemistry, you must not be solicitous (热切的) to *fill him with* information, but you must be careful that what he learns he knows of his own knowledge. Don't be satisfied with telling him that a magnet attracts iron. Let him see that it does; let him feel the pull of the one upon the other for himself.

9 And, especially, tell him that it is his duty to doubt until he is compelled, by the absolute authority of Nature, to believe that which is written in books. Pursue this discipline carefully and *conscientiously*, and you may make sure that, however scanty may be the measure of information which you have poured into the boy's mind, you have created an intellectual habit of priceless value in practical life.

10 One is constantly asked, when should this scientific education be commenced? I should say with the dawn of intelligence. As I have already said, a child seeks for information about matters of physical science as soon as it begins to talk. The first teaching it wants is an object-lesson of one sort or another; and as soon as it is fit for systematic instruction of any kind, it is fit for a modicum of science.

11 In these times the educational tree seems to me to have its roots in the air, its leaves and flowers in the ground; and, I *confess*, I should very much like to turn it upside down, so that its roots might be solidly *embedded* among the facts of Nature, and draw thence a sound nutriment for the *foliage* and fruit of literature and of art. No educational system can have a claim to *permanence*, unless it recognizes the truth that education has two great ends to which everything else must be *subordinated*. The one of these is to increase knowledge; the other is to develop the love of right and the hatred of wrong. With wisdom and *uprightness* a nation can make its way *worthily* and beauty will follow in the footsteps of the two.

New Words

constitute	[ˈkɑːnstətuːt]	v.	to be considered to be sth. 被视为;可算作
urge	[ɜːrdʒ]	v.	to strongly suggest that someone does sth. 催促;推进
conceive	[kənˈsiv]	v.	to imagine a particular situation or to think about sth. in a particular way 想象,设想
mischievous	[ˈmɪstʃəvəs]	a.	causing trouble or quarrels deliberately 恶意的;不友善的
possess	[pəˈzɛs]	v.	to have a particular quality or ability 具备,具有(特定品质、才能等)
discipline	[ˈdɪsəplɪn]	v.	to teach someone to obey rules and control their behavior 训练,训导
acquaint	[əˈkwent]	v.	to deliberately find out about sth. 使认识,使了解
approximation	[əˌprɑːksɪˈmeɪʃn]	n.	sth. that is similar to another thing, but not exactly the same 接近;近似
geology	[dʒiˈɑːlədʒi]	n.	the study of the rocks, soil etc. that make up the Earth, and of the way they have changed since the Earth was formed 地质学

Unit 8

preliminary	[prɪˈlɪmɪnəri]	a.	designed to orient or acquaint with a situation before proceeding 初步的，初级的
faculty	[ˈfækəlti]	n.	a natural ability, such as the ability to see, hear, or think clearly 官能；能力
elementary	[ˌɛləˈmɛntəri]	a.	concerning the first and easiest part of a subject 基本的；初级的
systematic	[ˌsɪstəˈmætɪk]	a.	characterized by order and planning 有系统的，有规则的
pretense	[ˈpriˌtɛns]	n.	a way of behaving which is intended to make people believe sth. that is not true 借口
peculiarity	[pɪˌkjuliˈærɪti]	n.	sth. that is a feature of only one particular place, person, situation etc 独特之处，特性
apprehend	[ˌæprɪˈhɛnd]	v.	to understand sth. 了解，明白
inductive	[ɪnˈdʌktɪv]	a.	using known facts to produce general principles 归纳法的；归纳的
deductive	[dɪˈdʌktɪv]	a.	using the knowledge and information you have in order to understand or form an opinion about sth. 推论的，演绎的
ultimate	[ˈʌltəmɪt]	a.	furthest or highest in degree or order; utmost or extreme 最后的；最终的
yield	[jild]	v.	to produce a result, answer, or piece of information 产生，带来（收益或效益）
eminent	[ˈɛmənənt]	a.	bing famous and important 显赫的，卓越的
conscientiously	[kɑnʃɪˈɛnʃəsli]	ad.	with a lot of knowledge and attention 谨慎地，认真地
confess	[kənˈfɛs]	v.	to admit sth. that you feel embarrassed about 承认
embed	[ɛmˈbɛd]	v.	to make sth. a basic part of sth. else or to make it difficult to remove 使植根于；使难以消除
foliage	[ˈfoʊliɪdʒ]	n.	the leaves of a plant 植物的叶子（总称）
permanence	[ˈpɜːrmənəns]	n.	the property of being able to exist for an indefinite duration 永久，持久
subordinate	[səˈbɔːrdɪnət]	v.	to put someone or sth. in a less important position 使……居下位，使在次级
uprightness	[ˈʌpraɪtnəs]	n.	the quality of always behaving in an honest way 正直
worthily	[ˈwɜːrðɪli]	a.	the way of deserving to be thought about or treated in a particular way 可敬的；令人称许的

Phrases & Expressions

pass on	to tell someone a piece of information that someone else has told you 传递（信息）
be mixed up	consist of many different types of things or people 混淆；搅合
in virtue of	by means of or as a result of 凭借……的力量；由于
at one's own peril	with an intent to to do sth. that is dangerous or could cause people harm or problems 自冒风险
fill...with	to provide sth. that is needed or wanted but which has not been available or present before 提供

1. The text was adapted from *Science and Education*, a collection of Thomas Henry Huxley's speeches and essays addressed at intervals during more than thirty years, to widely distant and different hearers and readers.
2. Thomas Henry Huxley (1825—1895) was one of the intellectual giants of the nineteenth century. Largely self-taught, he rose from humble beginnings to become a celebrated biologist, teacher, and promoter of science. Of all his achievements, he is best remembered for his spirited defense of Charles Darwin's theory of evolution by natural selection. His staunch support has since earned him the nickname "Darwin's bulldog."

Task 1 Generating the Outline

Directions: Please identify the thesis of the passage and the main point of each paragraph, and then find out how these points develop the thesis. You may use the table below for your help.

The thesis	All students when leaving schools should possess _____ and have been disciplined _____.
Para. 1: The introduction	The speaker begins with the lecture by raising a question _____.
Para. 2: The explanation	The speaker goes further to explain _____.
Para. 3: The explanation	The preliminary stage of scientific education is _____.
Para. 4: The explanation	The stage that followed should be _____.
Para. 5: The explanation	The modicum of instruction offered by school education should be given to _____.
Para. 6: The explanation	The great peculiarity of scientific training lies in drawing conclusions _____.
Para. 7: The illustration	The lecturer illustrates _____.

Unit 8

Para. 8: The explanation	It's essential to make scientific training practical by giving reality to your teaching _____.
Para. 9: The illustration	The lecturer illustrates the way to guide the children to observe the relationship _____.
Para. 10: The explanation	The lecturer explains _____.
Para. 11: The conclusion	Educational system can have a claim to permanence if it recognizes the truth that _____.

Task 2 Understanding the Text

Directions: Please answer the following ten questions based on Text A.

1. What's the purpose of scientific education for school boys and girls? (Para. 2)
2. What's the first step to get every child instructed in scientific education? (Para. 2)
3. According to Huxley, what are the two kinds of physical science? How do you classify systematic botany and physics? (Para. 4)
4. Should preparatory scientific training abide by a certain principle? Why? (Para. 5)
5. According to the author, what's the great peculiarity of scientific training? (Para. 6)
6. How should a scholar behave in everyday life? (Para. 7)
7. What does the author mean by saying that we should give reality to our teaching by object lessons? (Para. 8)
8. How can we create an intellectual habit of priceless value in the boy's mind in practical life? (Para. 9)
9. When should be an appropriate time to commence the scientific education in children? (Para. 10)
10. On what condition can educational system claim permanence? (Para. 11)

Task 3 Vocabulary Building

Directions: Conversion is a word-formation process whereby a word of certain word-class is shifted into a word of another word-class without an addition of an affix, which is also called "functional shift" or "derivation by zero suffix". For example:

n.—v.

Please notify us of any change of **address**.

The next question to which I have to **address** myself is, what sciences ought to be thus taught?

a.—v.

These aims were **subordinate** to the main aims of the mission.

Education has two great ends to which everything else must be **subordinated**.

Now choose the words listed below and complete the following sentences with appropriate forms when necessary.

| attempt | grasp | discipline | parrot |
| smooth | narrow | round | sober |

1. He has no original opinions; he's just his boss' echo by _____ his superior's words.

2. A few objections have to be _____ away before we can start the project of building nuclear plants.
3. The police have _____ down their list of suspects who had committed the murder by undertaking years of investigation.
4. Weather conditions prevented them from _____ crossing the bridge.
5. A short opening paragraph enables the reader to _____ what the article is about.
6. After thinking about every potential consequence of his plan, he _____ up and decided to face up to the challenge.
7. Next week's performance of Victor Hugo's renowned work Les Miserables will _____ out the opera season.
8. Different cultures have different ways of _____ their children.

Task 4 Learning the Phrases

Directions: Please fill in the blanks of the sentences below with the phrases listed in the box. Change the forms if necessary. Notice that some phrases need to be used more than once.

| acquaint oneself with | draw...from | pass on |
| pour into | in virtue of | turn...upside down |

1. The fewer calories the body uses from food the more it must _____ your surplus body fat, so this adds up to faster weight loss.
2. This photograph on my desk is now an object for me _____ my perceiving experience.
3. It's not all good news for Pat Nevin, for his football world will _____ today when he is left out of Scotland's World Cup squad.
4. It is necessary to _____ the reader _____ a little of the previous involvements of Highlander in order to understand the basic idea which underlies its activities.
5. The real cause of the trouble is that parents and teachers always _____ to us, as children, what they themselves have been told, and this has been going on for hundreds, or even thousands of years.
6. He became a champion at last _____ his perseverance.
7. Employees must _____ themselves _____ their rights under the employment protection laws, such as the right to maternity leave.
8. Sometimes it was like a sit-com, where two characters refuse to speak directly to each other, always using a third party to _____ comments.
9. A stream of spontaneous desire and aversion continues to _____ the center of me, and I never cease to choose new ends from among its goals.
10. Scientists study facts, observe experiments, _____ experience, think empirically, cogitate inductively, analyze, finally construct hypotheses, theories, and general concepts.

Unit 8

Task 5 Studying the Sentence Structure

"Even if" in Adverbial Clause of Concession

Sentences from the text

I hope you will consider that the arguments I have now stated, even if there were no better ones, constitute a sufficient apology for urging the introduction of science into schools.

Directions: Please combine the two sentences together by using "Even if" in Adverbial Clause of Concession.

Tips

1. There are several conjunctions which can be used in Adverbial Clauses of Concession, such as although, even if/though, however, whatever, no matter (who, what, when, where);
2. When referred to the situations that are not true or unlikely to be true, subjective mood should be used;
3. Both subjunctive mood and indicative mood can be used based on different situations.

1. He gets accepted to Harvard, he won't be able to afford the tuition.
   _____.

2. He was not concerned that he might be considered by society as an unskilled 'yokel'. He was not aware of the opinion of the world outside.
   _____.

3. Many of them turned a deaf ear to his advice. They knew it to be valuable.
   _____.

4. He tried very hard. He never seems able to do the work satisfactorily.
   _____.

5. He will drive or take a taxi to attend the wedding ceremony. He will not be on time.
   _____.

Adverbial Clause of Purpose

Sentences from the text

I should very much like to turn it upside down, so that its roots might be solidly embedded among the facts of Nature.

Directions: Please combine the two sentences together by using Adverbial Clause of Purpose.

Tips:

1. "So that," "in order that," "lest," "for fear that," and "in case," can be used to create an adverbial Clause of Purpose.
2. Modal verbs such as "may," "might," "can," "could," "should" and etc. are often employed in the adverbial clause.

1. Everyone will lend a hand in the project. The work might be finished ahead of schedule.
   _____.

2. She didn't walk far in the forest. She was afraid of getting lost.

   _____.

3. John spoke through a microphone. He could be heard in every room.

   _____.

4. We have planned a variety of activities. There will be something catering to everyone.

   _____.

5. We decided against installing new heating apparatus. It will be too costly.

   _____.

Task 6　Paraphrasing Difficult Sentences

1. What I mean is, that no boy nor girl should leave school without possessing a grasp of the general character of science, and without having been disciplined, more or less, in the methods of all sciences.

   _____
   _____.

2. As the reasoning faculties of the child grow, and he becomes familiar with the use of the tools of knowledge—reading, writing, and elementary mathematics—he should pass on to what is, in the more strict sense, physical science.

   _____
   _____.

3. If scientific education is to be dealt with as mere bookwork, it will be better not to attempt it, but to stick to the Latin Grammar which makes no presence to be anything but bookwork.

   _____
   _____.

4. Pursue this discipline carefully and conscientiously, and you may make sure that, however scanty may be the measure of information which you have poured into the boy's mind, you have created an intellectual habit of priceless value in practical life.

   _____
   _____.

5. No educational system can have a claim to permanence, unless it recognizes the truth that education has two great ends to which everything else must be subordinated.

   _____
   _____.

Task 7　Summarizing the Text

Directions: Please summarize text A in 150 words. You may use the table in Task 1 to help you.

Unit 8

Task 8 Writing with Cause and Effect

Directions: Write a passage of two paragraphs to discuss the reasons why scientific instruction must be given to ensure real knowledge and practical discipline. In the first paragraph, you should summarize Huxley's general attitude towards scientific education. In the second paragraph, you should analyze the reasons behind. Your writing should be about 200 words. You may use what is provided in the box below to help you.

Tips

1. Cause-effect essays explore the reasons for something and examine the results of events or actions. In other words, a cause deals with the question "why" and an effect, the question "what if". In answering the former question we reason from effect back to cause, and for the latter, from cause forward to effect.
2. In writing cause-effect essays, some transitions can be used to refer to cause-effect relationships, such as because, since, so, as, accordingly, therefore, as a consequence and etc.

> Thomas Henry Huxley, one of the intellectual giants of the nineteenth century, celebrated biologist, teacher, and promoter of science had once claimed that all school boys and girls should possess a grasp of general character of science and have been disciplined in the methods of science. According to him, scientific instruction must be given to ensure real knowledge and practical discipline. In my opinion, Huxley's argument is well-justified/biased.
>
> There are several reasons behind which can account for the practical way of scientific instruction at school....

Part Three Reading and Speaking

Text B

Man or Machine? The Age of the Robot Blurs Sci-fi and Cutting-edge Science
Andrew Belonsky

From Marvel's Ultron to Obama's brain mapping project, science and fiction are breaking the barriers between man and machine

1 No sci-fi plot is as reliable as that of the *rebelling* robot. It's a story as old as digital time: the once promising but ultimately impetuous computer/child, realizing its *mortal* creators are at best obsolete (过时的) and at worst a *plight*, tries to *eradicate* humanity/father.

2 The first play to *feature* automatons, Czech playwright Karel Capek's 1920 piece *Rossum's Universal Robots* (R.U.R.), provided the template for the rotten robot, one used in movies, in books, on television and even music, as on The Flaming Lips 2002

album Yoshimi Battles the Pink Robots.

3   And of course comic books have mined the robot-versus-man myth, as in the latest Marvel Comics limited series, *The Age of Ultron*, a tale in which villain Ultron, terrorizing heroes since 1968, returns once again to kill his creator, which is halfway through a run that culminates in June. The series' writer, Brian Michael Bendis, says: "If you take out the homicidal(嗜杀成性的)robot aspect of it, it's the son who can't live up his father's expectations and the father who can't control his son."

4   It's all very Oedipal(有恋母情结的), *dramatic* and sometimes even funny: back in 1985, *at the height of* primetime soap trend, one of Ultron's victims likened the robot's patricidal(弑父的) *obsession* to the convoluted plots of Dynasty: "You all sound like a soap opera. Are you sure you don't want Blake Carrington too?!" The pop culture references have changed since then, but so too has technology, and the *punchline's* looking to some like something of the past.

5   *Autonomous* robots are no longer the far-off, far-out fantasies they were in 1920 or 1968 or 1985. The latest generation of computerized creations appears to be pulling us closer to the fearsome sounding Singularity, the theoretical point when, according to futurist Ray Kurzweil, artificial intelligence will *surpass* our own. *Jeopardy*-winning supercomputer Watson was only the beginning.

6   To *alarmists*, the rise of the machines must stoke inhuman levels of anxiety. And why not? Technology can be truly discomforting. The US government's top secret Darpa labs are currently improving robots' behavioral learning and anomaly detection programs, both of which will make them "smarter" and more efficient killing machines, *literally*; auto manufacturers are working on self-driving cars like those that run us down in Daniel H Wilson's predictably plotted thriller Robopocalypse; and just this month word spread that European researchers turned on Raputya, an "internet for computers" that bears an uncanny *resemblance* to Skynet, the fictional super-computer that *launched* Terminator *into* our pop culture landscape.

7   But to those who embrace technology, these *upgrades* aren't harbingers hell-bent on destroying human life. They're portals into a brighter human future. Such technoptimists believe that as computers *evolve*, so will we. Google Glass is but the beginning of how technology will be meshed onto our bodies. Researchers are already hyping "e-memory" implants that could make Total Recall a reality; and the US Food and Drug Administration recently approved *artificial* retinas that use video processors and electrodes give partial sight to the blind, just one of the many examples of how "you," the human, can *merge* with "them," the machines. Futurist Kurzweil believes that nanotechnology will be able to rebuild injured humans.

8   "It's not us versus them," he told the New York Times. "We've created these tools to overcome our limitations."

9   If that's the case, the most transcendental merger between man and machine will be between silicon chips and our own motherboard, the brain, a long misunderstood organ that's suddenly getting fresh attention. The US National Institutes of Health

hopes $3bn will help *lay out* the Brain Activity Map, a cartographical layout announced by Barack Obama this month that will *dwarf* the Human Genome Project in scope and size. The European Union is putting up over $1bn for a similar, 10-year undertaking unimaginatively called the Human Brain Project, and the NIH's other *expedition* into gray matter, the Human Connectome Project, recently released two terabytes of data, a sliver of the amount of data the brain could hold: 100 terabytes by some *estimates*. That's 104,857,600 megabytes. To give you an idea of how far away we are from finish: doctors have yet to completely map a mouse brain, or even a fruit fly's.

10   This is all very exciting for *advocates* of "mind uploading," a *fantastical*, as-of-now *hypothetical* process by which we would transfer our organic brains, including memories, personalities, tastes and proclivities(倾向)into artificial bodies, or at least disk drives. According to them, once we have a clearer map of the brain and its memory drives, we can use existing technology to freeze or otherwise *preserve* our brains, wait 100, 200 or even 1,000 years for science to *take its course* and be awakened in a future, our experiences uploaded into an artificial body.

11   Dr Ken Hayworth, a neuroscientist who maps fruit fly brains by day and *advocates for* the independent Brain Preservation Foundation by night, says such a process is the final frontier in breaking the barrier between man and machine. "Mind uploading technology is just breaking the barrier," he says. "If you're really jealous of what your avatar is doing, if you're really jealous of your computer's memory, then mind uploading is the logical conclusion; it's saying: 'Okay, I won't beat them, I'll join them.'"

12   But if we join them, are we still human? Or will we become the creatures we have for so long feared and so far only fictionalized: superior beings who see organic, naturally born humans as ill-equipped competition? And, more importantly how expensive will analysis be?

New Words

rebell	[ri'bel]	v.	to oppose or fight against someone in a position of authority 反抗；造反
mortal	['mɔ:tl]	a.	not living forever 终有一死的
plight	[plaɪt]	n.	a situation from which extrication is difficult esp. an unpleasant or trying one 困境；苦境
eradicate	[ɪ'rædɪkeɪt]	v.	to completely get rid of sth. such as a disease or a social problem 摧毁；根除
feature	['fi:tʃə(r)]	v.	to show a particular person or thing in a movie, magazine, show etc. 以……为主要内容；特写

dramatic	[drəˈmætɪk]	a.	sudden, surprising and often impressive 突然的；惊人的
obsession	[əbˈseʃn]	n.	an extreme unhealthy interest in sth. or worry about sth., which stops you from thinking about anything else 痴迷；迷恋
punchline	[ˈpʌntʃlaɪn]	n.	the words at the end of a joke or story that make it funny, surprising, etc.(笑话结尾处的)包袱,妙语
autonomous	[ɔːˈtɑːnəməs]	a.	having the ability to work and make decisions by yourself without any help from anyone else 自主的
surpass	[səˈpɑːs]	v.	to be even better or greater than someone or sth. else 超过；优于
jeopardy	[ˈdʒepərdi]	n.	a source of danger; a possibility of incurring loss or misfortune 危险；危难
alarmist	[əˈlɑːmɪst]	n.	someone who makes people feel worried about dangers that do not really exist 危言耸听的人；杞人忧天的人
literally	[ˈlɪtərəli]	ad.	according to the most basic or original meaning of a word or expression 确实地；真正地
resemblance	[rɪˈzembləns]	n.	similarity between two things, especially in the way they look 相似；类似
upgrade	[ˌʌpˈgreɪd]	n.	sth. as a piece of equipment, that serves to improve or enhance 改良；更新
evolve	[iˈvɑːlv]	v.	to develop and change gradually over a long period of time 发展,演化
artificial	[ˌɑːrtɪˈfɪʃl]	a.	not real or not made of natural things but made to be like sth. that is real or natural 人造的
merge	[mɜːrdʒ]	v.	to combine, or to join things together to form one thing (使)合并；(使)融合
dwarf	[dwɔːrf]	v.	to be so big that other things are made to seem very small 使相形见绌
expedition	[ˌekspɪˈdɪʃən]	n.	a long and carefully organized journey, especially to a dangerous or unfamiliar place 远征；探险
release	[rɪˈliːs]	v.	to let news or official information be known and printed 发布；发表
estimate	[ˈestəˌmet]	n.	a calculation of the value, size, amount etc. of sth. 估算；估价
advocate	[ˈædvəˌket]	n.	someone who publicly supports someone or sth. 提倡者；支持者
fantastical	[fænˈtæstɪkəl]	a.	strange, unreal, and magical 空想的,捕风捉影的
hypothetical	[ˌhaɪpəˈθetɪkl]	a.	based on a situation that is not real, but that might happen (基于)假设的；假定的

Unit 8

| preserve | [prɪˈzɜːrv] | v. | to save sth. or someone from being harmed or destroyed 保持，维持（原状） |

Phrases & Expressions

at the height of	during a period of great prosperity 在鼎盛时期
launch...into	to start sth., usually sth. big or important 开始
lay out	to spend money, especially a lot of money 花（大钱）
take/run its course	develop in the usual way and reach a natural end 按照正常（本身）的程序进行
advocate for	to publicly say that sth. should be done 提倡；主张

1. This passage was published in the section of Science by *the Guardian* on Apr. 24, 2013.
2. Andrew Belonsky is a journalist based in New York. He writes for *Out and Towleroad*. He has contributed to the *New York Times*.
3. Ultron is a fictional character that appears in comic books published by Marvel Comics. The character first appeared in Avengers #54 (1968), and was created by writer Roy Thomas and artist John Buscema. In 2009, Ultron was ranked as IGN's 23rd Greatest Comic Book Villain of All Time.
4. Obama's brain mapping project is a decades-long project promoted by the president designed to map the inner workings of the brain, seeking answers to such challenges as epilepsy（癫痫）, autism（自闭症）and Alzheimer's disease（阿尔兹海默症）.

Task 1　Summarizing

Directions: Fill in the blanks in the following text outline with key points based on an overall understanding and then make an oral summary.

I. The robot-versus-man myth in science fiction
  a. The reliable sci-fi plot is that of a rebelling robot who _____.
  b. The template for the rotten robot _____.
  c. Some typical pop culture references such as _____ and _____.
  d. Conclusion: _____.

II. People's attitude towards machines or technology
  a. Cons: To alarmists, _____
  b. Pros: To advocates, _____.
    Applications and functions:
    1) _____; 2) _____; 3) nanotechnology

　　　　Outcome: We've created these tools to ＿＿＿＿＿＿ such as the most transcendental
　　　　　　　merger between man and machine in ＿＿＿＿＿＿ by Barack Obama.
　　　　Conclusion: Mind uploading technology is ＿＿＿＿＿＿＿＿＿＿＿＿＿＿＿＿＿＿.
III.　The author's standpoint:
　　　The author stands on the negative side by thinking that ＿＿＿＿＿＿＿＿＿＿＿＿＿＿＿.

Task 2　Reflecting on the Text

Directions: Now you've read the passage about the relationship between man and machine in the age of the robot. What do you think of the new type of relationship? What do you think of the rebelling robot in science fictions? Do you believe that artificial intelligence will surpass human brain? Is it a good thing that uploading technology is breaking the barrier between man and machine? Will we become the creatures we have for so long feared? Exchange views with your partner. You may include the following points in your discussion.

The robot-versus-man myth in science fiction
The traditional pop culture references—rotten robots
Alarmists' views on technology
Advocates' views on technology
The examples of the merger between man and machine
The author's opinion on the most transcendental merger between man and machine
Your own standpoints

Task 3　Making a Presentation

Directions: Give an oral presentation of your views on such topics as "Artificial intelligence will surpass our own" and "The Google Glass is a blessing to make life more convenient." You should state your view clearly in the beginning, and then use your interview data and other sources to support your points.

1. Artificial intelligence will surpass our own。
2. The Google Glass is a blessing to make life more convenient

> 1) Recent years have seen dramatic gains in...
> 2) an electronic super-intelligence
> 3) outstrip/surmount human performance
> 4) evolution of robots
> 5) world-changing breakthroughs
> 6) technology being viewed as the instructor
> 7) merge into
> 8) be subject to
> 9) assist in
> 10) a series of sophisticated analysis and scientific researches
> 11) It may well be that...
> 12) as unimaginable to us as opera is to a flatworm

Part Four Cross Cultural Communication

Passage A

万世师表，以德服人

孔子，名丘，字仲尼，春秋末期鲁国人，是我国伟大的思想家、教育家。

孔子的思想以"仁"为核心，他认为"仁"即"爱人"，仁，即是做人的道理。"仁者人也"，做一个人需要能尽人道，便是仁。因此，孔子提出了"己所不欲，勿施于人"的观点，即自己都不希望别人这样对待自己，那就不要以同样的言行对待他人。

这就是所谓的"恕"。从积极方面说，就是自己有某种要求需要满足，也要推想他人也有这种要求需要满足。"己欲立而立人，己欲达而达人"，这也就是所谓"忠"。综合来讲，"忠恕之道"正是孔子推行为人之方。曾子说："夫子之道，忠恕而已矣。"忠恕之道说起来很容易，实行起来困难，因为人们都是有欲望的，常常把自己的利益放在第一位……

孔子首创私人讲学风气，主张"有教无类""因材施教""学而不厌，诲人不倦"的教学态度，强调"学"与"思"的重要性，总结出"学而不思则罔，思而不学则殆"和"温故而知新"等有效的学习方法。

他认为，学习时，首先应该采取虚心的、实事求是的老实态度；"知之为知之，不知为不知，是知也"；其次学习的知识面要广泛，学习的途径也要多样化；同时，学与思两者缺一不可。有学无思，只可记得许多没有头绪条理的物事，算不得知识。有思无学，便没有思的材料，知识胡思乱想，也算不得知识。

在天道观上，孔子不否认天命鬼神的存在，但又对其持怀疑态度，主张"敬鬼神而远之"。他认为"不知命，无以为君子也"。孔子宣扬天命论，他说："君子有三畏，畏天命，畏大人，畏圣人之言。"他把天命、大人、圣人之言并列起来，认为三者都是可敬畏的，人的生死、贫富，以及成功、失败，都是由天命决定的，承认有天命，顺天命而行，就不需要求鬼神的帮助保护了。

孔子说："吾十有五而志于学，三十而立，四十而不惑，五十而知天命，六十而耳顺，七十而从心所欲，不逾矩。"孔子活了72岁，这段话讲了他70岁以后的精神境界："从容中道，生日也。"也就是说他的精神完全达到了自觉的程度。

孔子有诸多建树，他整理了《诗经》《尚书》等古代文献，并删定《礼经》《乐经》，为《周易》作序，还编修了鲁国史官所记的《春秋》。相传孔子先后有弟子三千人，其中著名贤人者七十二。《论语》一书，便记载了他和这些弟子的对话问答，成为研究中国古代哲学的重要史料。

自西汉以后，孔子的学说成为两千多年封建社会的文化正统，影响深远。他在世时已被世人认为是当时社会上最博学者之一，赞誉其为"天纵之圣""千古圣人"，后世又尊称其为"至圣"——圣人之中的圣人、万世师表。

1. 本篇节选北京联合出版公司2014年1月出版的《北大哲学课》。该书包括哲学与西方哲学两部分,以北大著名哲学教授们的教学指导为方向。本文主要是对孔子生平、教育理念和方法的介绍。
2. 编者主要由国内知名高校教授和讲师组成。

Word Bank

万世师表	an exemplary teacher for all ages
实事求是	be practical and realistic
仁	benevolence
天命论	Confucius fatalism
忠恕之道	the doctrine of loyalty and consideration for others
不逾矩	without trespassing what is right
有教无类	teaching without distinction of classes
弟子	disciple
因材施教	teaching students in accordance with their aptitude
文化正统	orthodox culture

Directions: Please summarize the passage in English. Your summary should be about 150-200 words.

Passage B

The Socratic Quest for Wisdom

Martin Cohen

Socrates was a pretty amazing example of a person living the search for wisdom. He himself did not leave any writings. He did his philosophizing orally, in the company of other people—and not always in the company of people who were enjoying the journey with him. As he went about Athens questioning reputedly wise people on topics of importance and finding them not so wise after all, he insisted on pointing this fact out to them. And this proclivity, as you can well imagine, did not lead to widespread popularity.

Many of the young people in Athens were impressed with Socrates' razor-sharp intellect and often followed him about, imitating his probing style of conversation and offending even more people. In fact, by the age of 70, Socrates and his followers angered so many prominent citizens in Athens that he was accused and tried on the two trumped-up charges of corrupting the youth and of not believing in the gods of the city but following other gods instead.

Plato provides a riveting account of the trial of Socrates. His fate was in the hands of a crowd of 501 citizen-jurists, who were to weigh the evidence and decide his fate by vote. The evidence seems clear that, if Socrates had just promised to stop philosophizing in public and stirring up trouble, he'd most likely have been freed. In his speech to the jurists, he considered this possibility and said that, if

Unit 8

the offer were made, his response would be simple. His words ring through the centuries. He said that his reply would be as follows:

Gentlemen of the jury, I am grateful and I am your friend, but I will obey the god rather than you, and as long as I draw breath and am able, I shall never cease to practice philosophy, to extort you and in my usual way to point out to any of you whom I happen to meet: Good Sir, you are an Athenian, a citizen of the greatest city with the greatest reputation for both wisdom and power; are you not ashamed of your eagerness to possess as much wealth, reputation, and honor as possible, while you do not care for nor give thought to wisdom or truth, or the best possible state of your soul?

He went on to say:

Then, if one of you disputes and says he does care, I shall not let him go at once or leave him, but I shall question him, examine him and test him, and if I do not think he has attained the goodness that he says he has, I shall reproach him because he attaches little importance to the most important things and greater importance to inferior thins, I shall treat in this way anyone I happen to meet, young and old, citizen and stranger, and more so the citizens because you are more kindred to me. Be sure that this is what the god orders me to do, and I think there is no greater blessing for the city than my service to the god. For I go around doing nothing but persuading both young and old among you not to care for your body or your wealth in preference to or as strongly as for the best possible state of your soul, but I say to you: "Wealth does not bring about excellence, but excellence brings about wealth and all other public and private blessings for men."

Wisdom is worth the pursuit. Yet, despite its enormous relevance in helping us to live good lives, nothing may be as rare in the modern world as true wisdom.

Former U.S President Calvin Coolidge once remarked that "Some people are suffering from lack of work, some from lack of water, many more from lack of wisdom." And one can make the same point even more strongly today.

Although it's sometimes considered nothing more than enhanced common sense, nothing may be less common in our time than real wisdom about living. We should seek as much as we can to enhance the wisdom we have, by exploring all the ultimate issues most fundamental to our understanding of life and our place in the world.

Is the search for wisdom worth your time? Socrates thought that it was worth his life.

 Notes

1. The passage was adapted from *Philosophy for Dummies* which covers key philosophers, philosophical history and theory and the big questions that affect us today. It introduces Socratic quest for wisdom and probing style of conversation.
2. Martin Cohen is a philosophy author who has written numerous books, including *101 Philosophical Problems* and *101 Ethical Dilemmas*. Martin is the Editor of The Philosopher, one of the UK's oldest philosophy journals.

Directions: Please summarize the passage in Chinese. Your summary should be about 200—300 words.